24 Hour Telephone Renewals 0845 071 4343

HARINGEY LIBRARIES

THIS BOOK MUST BE RETURNED ON OR BEFORE
THE LAST DATE MARKED BELOW

To	HORNSEY LIBRARY	
−7 DEC 2015 3014		
1 8 JUN 2016 −9 MAY 2018 −9 MAY 2018 1 4 JUL 2018 13·3·20		

Online renewals – visit libraries.haringey.gov.uk

published by Haringey Council's Communications Unit 973.16 • 08/12

Live the Life You Love at 50+
A handbook for career and life success

Keren Smedley

Mc
Graw
Hill
Education

McGraw-Hill Education
McGraw-Hill House
Shoppenhangers Road
Maidenhead
Berkshire
England
SL6 2QL

world wide web: www.mcgraw-hill.co.uk

and Two Penn Plaza. New York, NY 10121-2289, USA

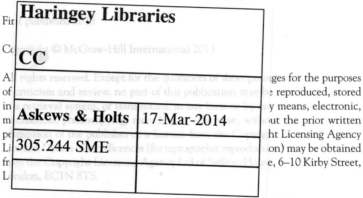

Fir[st published] [...]

Co[pyright] © McGraw-Hill International 2013

Al[l] rights reserved. Except for the quotation of short [passa]ges for the purposes
of [cr]iticism and review, no part of this publication ma[y b]e reproduced, stored
in [a retr]ieval system, or tran[smitted in any form or by an]y means, electronic,
m[...] [...]ise, with[o]ut the prior written
pe[rmission of the publication] [...] [Copyrig]ht Licensing Agency
Li[mited] licenc[e (for reprographic reproduc]on) may be obtained
fr[om the Copyright Licensing Agency Limited of Saffron Ho]e, 6–10 Kirby Street,
L[on]don, EC1N 8TS.

A catalogue record of this book is available from the British Library

ISBN-13: 978-0-07-714597-2

Library of Congress Cataloging-in-Publication Data
CIP data to come

Typeset by Aptara, Inc.
Printed in Great Britain by CPI

To the clients who have made this book possible

Praise for this Book

"They say 50 is the new 30, and most of us would love to embrace this concept, if only we had a guide to mentor us along the way. With insight, positivity, and brimming with practical ideas and solutions, this book shows us how reaching for the stars at 50+, fulfilment wise, is both achievable and empowering."

Jo Hemmings,
Behavioural Psychologist and Relationship Coach

"Leading a busy professional career often doesn't provide the opportunity to take stock of one's overall life – and at 50 there's more than half of your adult life left to live! Live the Life you Love at 50+ provides some excellent context around the changes to modern family living and practical guidance on how to get the most out of life. Keren writes in a friendly style that encourages you to examine what you are about and challenges you to take control of your life. I would recommend this book to any 50-something starting to think about what they do next – or those who act as line manager, mentor or coach to individuals who need to address this challenge."

Martin Ellis,
Partner, *Grant Thornton UK LLP*

"This excellent book is full of ideas to start afresh and develop a positive outlook on life. Course participants share their challenges and this helps the reader to reflect on their own circumstances. It prepares the reader for their future."

Professor Stephen Palmer PhD,
***Centre for Coaching,* London, UK**

"When I awoke the morning I turned 60, I felt triumphant. I felt new energy and confidence. I could not wait to get started living this decade. I did not expect that. Keren's new book has just explained why. In her warm counterpoint of story, introspection, theory and data Keren offers us a real understanding of how life can be, is meant to be, from 50 onwards. She is ruthless with negative myths. She is irrepressible with exciting (and achievable) possibilities. And she is practical, expecting you to be, too. Throughout, you feel she is with you, right there knowing, listening, teaching, even beaming. All of us over 50 should read it and do what she proposes. So should everyone on the way to 50 for that matter."

Nancy Kline,
Time to Think Coaching, UK

"Short on waffle, long on research, Keren's book is crammed with useful information, suggestions and practical tools and exercises. This guide will help anyone in the 'second act' of their lives to reach their full potential."

Tim Willis,
Editor, *High50.com*

Acknowledgements

This book could not have been written without the support and help I've had from a number of people. Richard Barber has been behind me all the way ensuring the prose flowed; Kathy Reddington has supported, encouraged, and advised me without a grumble; and Martin Gelgyn has cooked delicious, sustaining meals and managed two house moves for us without complaining that I was at my desk!

I'd also like to thank Patti Barber and Alarys and Chris Gibson for so kindly offering their homes for me to write in; Debra Jinks for reading the book and offering me really valuable feedback; Nancy Kline for her positive words; and Val Hudson for her advice.

Many thanks, too, to my editor Monika Lee who immediately saw that a coaching book for this age group was what many of us needed.

Finally, and by no means least, a big thank you to my clients and course participants who so generously allowed me to use their stories in this book. I have learnt so much from them about how to grow older gracefully and manage the hurdles along the way.

Contents

Part IV
Your Health and Wellbeing

About the Author

Keren Smedley is an experienced life and business coach who has established herself as one of the UK's most sought after commentators on relationship issues: whether personal or within the workplace. She is the Woman's Weekly Agony aunt and BBC Berkshire relationship expert. Keren writes regularly for the Daily Mail and contributes to The Sun, Good Housekeeping and Woman and Home.

Introduction

There are abundant numbers of books for sale that offer us, whatever our age, the opportunity to scale great heights, overcome any difficulties we might have, reach for the sky, ensure all our dreams come true, and so on. The list is endless. Yet here you are reading this introduction. I wonder what it is that draws you here? I expect you are 'of an age' or know someone who is and wondered what was on offer.

You may have read the title and thought, 'That's just what I want and, if all I need to do is read that book, it's worth a try.' Or you may be much more cynical and think, 'That's so unlikely but let's see if there's anything of value in there.' Or you may be searching because you are a bit stuck and you are no longer having such a great time at 50, 60 or 70.

You might be a coach or counsellor who has clients who are of this age and you need a few more ideas, or you could just be curious, as you know there is always more to learn. I do not mind the reason. I am just pleased you are here. And you have come to the right place.

This is a coaching book both for individuals and for coaches. What does that mean and how will this differ from other self-help books? We all have hidden potential and talents that are lurking beneath the surface. The tricky thing is to know how to unearth them. Coaching is the ideal way.

For example, sports coaches help athletes to build on their skills by enabling them to define their goals, identify the skills required to achieve them, assess where they need to improve if they are going to meet these goals, and create an action plan to get there. They then encourage the athletes, praise them, point out areas for improvement, and get them to work hard to reach their targets.

This is exactly what you are going to be doing if you engage with this book. As your own coach, you will have the opportunity to identify who you want to be, identify your values and beliefs, create a personal vision for your life, and develop the skills and strategies to do so while encouraging and praising yourself all the way! Coaching enables people to meet their desires quickly, simply, and easily.

As a coach, you will need to monitor your thoughts and feelings so that you can make significant changes. As you go through this book, you will also need to jot down the answers to some of the questions and exercises you come across. I suggest you get a dedicated notebook in which to write your answers and to which you can refer back to. Give each questionnaire and exercise a title or jot down the page in the book you are referring to so that you can easily cross-reference when required. Unlike in school, coaching has no right answers. Each answer is your own and so is 100 per cent right for you. A real plus about being your own coach is that no one will read your answers unless you choose to share them, so you have a licence to be as open and honest as you want without any fear of anyone challenging you.

But I must be very clear with you. Just reading this book will not be all that is needed to make a difference. You will need to want to make some changes in your life and be willing to lose limiting beliefs as well as develop new skills and coping strategies. You will need to be motivated to want to change. If you are half-hearted about it, you won't get far.

You will also need to believe that change is possible. And you must give me the benefit of the doubt that I can offer you things that will help you to have the life you want. Practice does indeed make perfect and you will have to push yourself even if the going gets a bit tough. You may also have to examine some of the ways you behave, as they may no longer be useful for you.

Once you have mastered it all, I cannot pretend there'll never be a bad day when things will appear to go backwards or periods when you will be unhappy with your life or feel stuck. If you follow your chosen exercises, what I can guarantee is that you will have the skills and wherewithal to know how to manage those times better and how to move yourself to a better place quicker.

Assuming that you are still reading, and before you go any further, I would like you to stop and answer some initial questions. So get your notebook out!

 Ask yourself
- How would you describe your life at the moment? Score it from 1 to 10 (with 10 being fabulous and 1 being awful).
- How are you feeling? Again score it.
- What made you pick this book up?
- What are the immediate things that come to mind you want to change?
- What are you hoping to gain?
- What would make this the most useful book ever for you?

As you are reading the book or doing the exercises, you need to keep those initial answers in mind so that everything you do is with the purpose of meeting those desires and improving your scores.

That is the first coaching lesson: doing things with purpose will deliver you your dreams. Too often we just do what we do without knowing why we are doing it and, not surprisingly, we do not always get what we want!

So you now know what you are doing here. Let me tell you what I am doing here, too, and why I wanted to write this book. It is important that you know as we make this journey together.

A few years ago, when I had just turned 50, I was sitting talking to a friend about our lives. We were not discontent but it was clear to both of us that life had not turned out as we had expected when we had been playing at being 'grown-ups' as children. Of course, no one really expects they will be the prince or princess they dreamt of, but I did think life would follow a similar path to that of my parents.

I was born in the 1950s into a traditional family where my father worked full-time and my mother, after both her children began attending primary school, worked part-time. Even that was fairly unusual, as most mothers stayed at home. Education was important to my parents, so I was encouraged to stay on at school but with the expectation that I would, when I married, work part-time and be supported by my husband.

Many of my female contemporaries left school at 16 and started working while looking for a husband. Young men expected to find jobs and support their families while household chores and bringing up the children were left on the whole to their wives. By the time I was in my late teens, the Beat generation, free love, and women's lib were high on the agenda and my childhood expectations had already changed. Fundamentally, though, the beliefs and values to which I had been conditioned were still in place and they have remained the building blocks for my adult life.

Divorce was rare so I had assumed I would stay married to the same man. I would probably take time off when my children were small and then return to work part-time. My children would be educated, find good jobs, afford to live in their own homes, and live independently from 21 at the latest. I never considered a parent having dementia and all the stress and pain that causes, and I had also not expected to be someone's child until I was well into my fifties.

Has life turned out for you as you expected? It may be far better than you ever dreamt, or some elements may be, whereas other aspects have not lived up to expectation. We will look at this further in Chapter 3.

Our generation has not done life the way our parents did for lots of reasons. Women are back in the workplace, men have become been more involved in childrearing, many of our children cannot support themselves and are part of the 'boomerang generation', our parents have lived much longer, with dementia not being unusual, divorce and step-parenting are common, our pensions won't keep us in our dotage, there is no retirement age, and the increase in life expectancy means that we may well live until we are into our nineties!

This world is new, exciting and scary, and we do not have a blueprint for going forward. We are making it up as we go along, which is great if we have got a clear vision of where we want to go. It is not so useful if we are undirected and find ourselves in a cul-de-sac unable to get out.

I have worked in the field of therapy and people development for nearly 30 years and, the more I talk to others who are of a similar age, the clearer it is to me that my friend and I are not alone in our concerns. Most of us are wondering how to navigate the next 20 or 30 years. We need help but there is very little out there for us to turn to.

Of course, how we look is important to us, just as how fit we are, but for most of us it is the more fundamental issues that we need to explore. I have become passionate in helping others like me to make the right choices so we achieve a good and fulfilling last third of our lives.

Bronnie Ware is an Australian nurse who spent several years working in palliative care, caring for patients in the last 12 weeks of their lives. In her book *The Top Five Regrets of the Dying* she recounts that the first regret of her interviewees is, 'I wish I'd the courage to live a life true to myself, not the life others expected of me'.[1] Well, it is never too late to do so and this book will help you to do just that. Age no longer defines what you can or cannot do; it does, however, have an impact on your choices.

This book will explore the issues facing the 50+ 'baby boomer' generation and look at how to overcome the difficulties they encounter. You will find new insights and strategies that will enable you to live the life you want and be able to do what you want to do. You will find numerous solutions to help you shift any worries and concerns and live life to the full and enjoy it.

Although written for individuals, this book can be easily used by a coaching professional to highlight the issues as well as gain insight and information, and includes exercises that can be used in a coaching session. Each chapter outlines the issues, uses case studies as examples, and offers tips, ideas and exercises for the individual to use at their leisure or coaches to use in their sessions.

It also introduces you to different psychological models and theories to enable you to understand yourself better. You will be able to connect, through the case studies and examples, to others who are facing the same dilemmas. You will realize you are not alone and that some of your issues spring from the way the world is now, not because you have 'done it wrong'. Knowing that it is not your 'fault' is a really good place to start. It will increase your confidence and help to move you into a better frame of mind where you can begin to make the necessary changes.

This book is divided into four parts and then subdivided into thirteen chapters. The chapters can be read in any order. They can be chosen in order of relevance to you. Sometimes there will be references to ideas and models explained earlier in the book, as all the topics are interrelated. So you may need to move around a bit. If you follow the exercises that relate to your circumstances and interests, you will feel different and be really well equipped to *live the life you love at 50+* and be truly successful in whatever you choose to do.

Now it is down to you.

Part I
The Big Question

Chapter One
Know Yourself Now

Marion, 55

Marion is 55 and came to see me because she was fed up with her life. It just wasn't quite what she'd expected. She expected that by 55 her life would be easy. She would probably not be working and her husband would be earning enough to support her and her family. If she were working it would be because she wanted to rather than out of necessity. On the surface, there was nothing that seemed that bad. She was in a full-time job because she needed to work but she enjoyed it most of the time. She had divorced her first husband and was now in a pretty good long-term relationship with no more than the normal ups and downs. Her children had been through a hard time when her marriage had broken down but things were easier now. The children saw their father regularly and were doing what was expected for young people of their age. Her elderly parents were both still alive. They were a worry for her as she wasn't sure what the future held. She felt guilty about feeling disgruntled because, compared to most, she had a good life. She felt stuck and in a rut. She felt as though she had been on a treadmill for a long time and that she was often just running round to make sure everyone else's life was functioning. During the difficult years after her divorce she had struggled to make ends meet but she was through that now. She arrived for her first session embarrassed that she was there at all, as she felt it was a bit self-indulgent.

But she knew that things weren't quite right and that another 30 years of life like this would be seriously unfulfilling.

Marion, like many of us in our fifties and sixties, is living a very different life from the one she imagined. When we're young, we create a picture of our future from watching our parents and other adults and listening to the expectations they have for us. The books and magazines we read also influence us, as do the television programmes we watch. This image will include our beliefs and values about how things should be. Over the years we forget that this is a fantasy and not a reality, so when it does not happen because the world has moved on, we feel disappointed.

Not all the beliefs we held when we were young are useful to us as adults. This chapter will offer you an opportunity to examine your beliefs and decide whether they are outdated and need a bit of a revamp so they can serve you well in the future and not hinder your progress.

I put to Marion the initial questions I asked you in the Introduction (see p. 3). If you have not answered these, please go back and do so. I then asked her a series of further questions, which I want you to answer, too. You may not be fed up like Marion but, for many of us, our lives are not like we dreamt they'd be when we were children playing 'grown-ups'. Get your notebook out!

Ask yourself
 – When you say your life is not as you expected, I assume you have a picture in your mind of what it was meant to look like? Take a look at the picture and just imagine it.
 – Write about or draw that life – make it as detailed as you can.

- Who would be there?
- What would you be doing?
- What would be important to you in your life?
- What would your beliefs and values be?
- What would others be doing that they're not doing now?
- Where would you be living?
- Would you be working, and, if so, doing what – full- or part-time?
- What would you be doing for leisure?
- What would your dreams and aspirations be?
- Why is it so disappointing that it is not like that?
- What things are you missing out on?

Marion was unable to answer all the questions before we did some more exercises, which appear later in this chapter. You may find these useful, too. What was so interesting was that the life she imagined she'd have was based on her childhood memories. She went straight back to that world adding a few mod cons like a dishwasher and the Internet.

Early childhood influences

Many of us will agree that our early childhood experiences influence our lives. This is reflected in the Jesuit saying, 'Give me a child until he is seven and I will give you the man', which is based on a quotation by Ignatius Loyola.[1]

To really understand ourselves and what has influenced us, it's worth taking a look at life at that age. Although Marion liked her job well enough, she had not expected either to need to work full-time to make ends meet or to be working full-time. Her mother had not worked outside the home after she had children. Marion is not alone in thinking like this.

Life in the old days!

Marion is one of the 21 million 'baby boomers' living in the UK. We were born between 1946 and 1964. This was a period of rapid social change. Early baby boomers had a different start to life and expectations from those born near the end of the period in 1960. For early boomers, there was an assumption that boys would do National Service, which finished at the end of 1960 with the last serviceman being demobilized in 1963. The men would be the breadwinners and were expected to work to provide for their families. In 1953, in a popular book of advice for women entitled *Speaking as a Woman*, Phyllis Whitman stated: 'A happy marriage may be seen, not as a holy state or something to which a few may luckily attain but rather as the best course, the simplest, and the easiest way of life for us all'.[2] However, over the next few years, girls were given increased educational opportunities and employment possibilities but career choices were limited for the majority. Most girls still believed they would work until they married, that they would have a job not a career, and that they might return part-time when their children were older. Talk to any young woman now and you would hear something very different. Their expectation is that they will have a career and a family if they want one and that they are of equal value in the workplace to any man and that this should be recognized through equal pay and conditions.

Defying the norm

I need to add a caveat here. There were of course people who defied the norm, such as the few women who became doctors or lawyers and the few men who stayed home to look after their children, but they were the exception to the rule. Between 1974 and 2000, there was a 200 per cent increase in the time that fathers actively engaged with their children (25 minutes a day compared with only 8 minutes in the 1970s). A survey of sixteen industrialized countries found time devoted to childcare by married fathers in full-time employment with children under 5 had risen from 0.4 hours per day in 1960 to 1.2 hours by 2000.[3]

Changes in women's working patterns

In the UK in the early 1950s, there was an image of a 'universal woman', who was white and middle-class, to which all women aspired. This becomes very clear if you look at magazines of the time, such as *Woman's Weekly* and *Good Housekeeping*. But, by the end of the 1950s and early 1960s, things had begun to change and there was a steady rise in the number of women returning to paid work, albeit part-time for many, when their children were in school. Due to a shortage in the workplace, girls were encouraged to stay at school and become qualified. Some of the girls' mothers felt unfulfilled, as they had not had a career and they wanted their daughters to have a different experience. Mothers' employment tripled between 1951 and 2008, a trend that looks set to continue. The feminist movement that grew rapidly in the late 1960s campaigned for equal rights for women in education and in the workplace. It took a while for this to effect a significant change in the workplace. By 2008, around two-thirds of mothers were employed, with 38 per cent of mothers with dependent children working part-time. It is projected that by 2013, over 70 per cent of mothers will be in paid employment.[4] Having children is no longer seen as something that will reduce your career opportunities. However, we still have a way to go in my opinion, as in some professions it is not easy to work part-time or flexibly while your children are young and still get to the top in your profession.

Sally, 50

Sally came to see me to discuss her future career plans. She's a lawyer in a large City firm and she's a late baby boomer. Her 74-year-old mother had gone to university, which was fairly unusual, to study mathematics. She had met Sally's father while at university and they decided to marry. She left before completing her degree, as he didn't want her to be a student and her parents also thought she should devote her time to her husband. She had a good life and was frustrated that she had not pursued her passion. When her first daughter was born she was determined that Sally would not suffer the same fate. She put a lot of energy into her daughter's education and Sally became a successful lawyer. Fired with the same determination as her mother, she had managed, unlike many of her contemporaries, to have both a family and become a partner in the firm. She was aware that it had taken her a bit longer than it had her male counterparts and that she had missed out on a lot of her children's youth, as there was no flexibility and she'd had to return to work soon after their births and continue to work the long hours expected of her.

Relationships

When Marion and Sally were brought up, the expectation was that you married once, unless you were widowed, and even if it was not a very good relationship you made the best of it. Very few women divorced, and then only when in abusive relationships harmful to them and/or their children. The fantasy most of us grew up with was that we would get married 'and live happily ever after!' Although much happier in her second relationship, Marion had not anticipated her first one would fail. She'd always expected to be married 'until death us do part'. She had an acrimonious divorce and this had made things difficult for her and her children. She was really pleased to be in a fulfilling relationship but felt ambivalent about being divorced because it didn't fit with her values. She was brought up at a time when it was expected that men and women would marry and it was very unusual if you didn't. It didn't really matter how unhappy you were, you still stayed together. Our generation has changed this and it is now common for couples whose relationships are not working to separate and divorce. There is also a wide variety of different lifestyles, including co-habiting, civil partnerships, and being single, that are all seen by most as acceptable styles of modern living.

Beliefs

But although she lives in today's world where things are very different from her childhood, Marion's beliefs and values reside in her early life. It is almost always ideal for children to live with both parents. And yet, if you look at the figures, it increasingly is not the case, so Marion's level of embarrassment doesn't reflect today's society.

- First marriages have halved since 1970, whereas second and third marriages have doubled.
- In 1960, a divorce took place every 20 minutes. Since 1980, a divorce takes place every 3 minutes.
- In the 1950s, a million divorces would have taken 30 years; since 1980, a million divorces occur every 6 years.

- Divorce rates have been steady since 1980 but six times higher than they were in the 1950s.
- Couples living together before a first marriage rose from little more than 2 per cent at the end of the 1950s to 77 per cent by 1996, while the figures for co-habiting prior to a second marriage are even higher.
- Over a fifth of couples will be in a co-habiting relationship (as opposed to a marriage) by 2021 compared with 12 per cent of couples in 1996.
- By the year 2000, almost 40 per cent of births occurred outside marriage compared with only 5.6 per cent in 1950.
- The break-up rate for co-habiting relationships into which children are born has been estimated as being as high as 65 per cent.[5]

Change of views and beliefs

But the statistics alone certainly didn't change Marion's views and beliefs and they are unlikely to change yours. This is because our beliefs are not based on logical thinking. Many of us, including myself, live a very different life from the one we thought was mapped out for us. Much of it is considerably better as I am able to do things I never imagined I would. However, there are many times, such as coming home tired at the end of a long day at work, when I find myself thinking, 'this wasn't how I thought it would be'. Once we have a belief we find ways to reinforce it. We look for any evidence that we can find to prove our point! The following exercise, however, had a real effect on Marion. It is one you can follow, too. You will need your notebook.

Exercise: Changing negative beliefs

1. Write down a negative belief that is stopping you feeling good about yourself and your life – for example, 'I am a bad person because my marriage ended', 'I need to keep my divorce secret because it shows I am a failure', 'I shouldn't be expected to work at my age', or 'My partner has to work because I don't earn enough to keep my family so I am letting them down'.

2. What is it doing for you having these beliefs? Probably not a lot!

3. What is it doing for you thinking about it again and again? Again, I expect not a lot!

4. What evidence do you have to believe these are right?

5. One of the best ways to change a belief is to challenge it. For example:

   • Why do I think I am a bad person because my marriage ended?
   • Do I have any evidence to support this?
   • Did someone tell me I was bad? Why have I taken what they say to be the truth? Do I believe everything they say? Unlikely!
   • How many people said something different?

6. The more you challenge your beliefs, the less sense they make and the less power they have. Try doing this with other negative beliefs you have.

7. Now think about what you would like to believe instead? For example: 'I am a good person who was in the wrong marriage', 'There is no shame attached to being

divorced', 'It is good to work whatever our age, there is no age limit', or 'It is right that both of us support our family'. Write down your new beliefs.

8. When you articulate these, how do you feel? I expect a lot better.

9. Who is in control of your head and your thoughts? Yes, you!

10. Every time you find the negative thought/belief coming into your head, replace it with the positive one.

11. You have to do this every time a negative thought creeps in. If you do, you will find that the positive thought becomes your new habit.

If you are struggling to do this, every time the negative thought comes into your mind change the voice that says it into a silly one, such as a high-pitched squeak! Pretty quickly you will find that you can't take it seriously. (See Chapter 6 for more information on this.)

Reflection

How did you get on with this exercise? It is an essential so I recommend that you try it daily for a week and you will be amazed how things will change. The more you do this the more they will change. If you hold other negative beliefs about yourself, I suggest you do the same exercise again with them. The more positive we are about ourselves, the more likely we are to have good experiences.

Modern life

It is not just family life where things are different. Work, communication, travel, and technology are just a few of the others. We will continue this theme in the next few chapters. As coaches, while interested in the past up to a point, we are much more concerned about tackling the present. Knowing that Marion's fed up and that her family life and work are not as she expected is useful but not a solution. It is very easy for most of us to get fixated on a problem and talk about it all the time and yet do very little about it. Coaching is a useful way to stop that cycle and work with oneself to make a difference.

Looking forward

Dreaming is something all of us will have done since we were very young. We played with our dreams and thoughts when we indulged in make-believe. Most of us will have times as adults when we find ourselves somewhere else; we get caught up in a daydream, and having a dream or goal is essential if you are going to achieve what you want. Highly successful people will tell you that they had a dream or goal at the forefront of their mind and that this is what got them to where they are today. The next exercise is very useful and, like the belief exercise, is fundamental – so you need to give it a go.

Get your notebook ready, as you will need to jot a few things down.

Exercise: Future perfect

1. Imagine a line in front of you that starts when you were born and stretches until you are 90 or 100. See it divided into 10-year blocks.

2. Stand at the end of the first stretch, 0–10 years. Imagine walking along the line slowly remembering all the things that happened to you. Just allow your thoughts to flow

freely. It doesn't matter how much or little you recall. When you get to 10, fold up that bit of the line and start again with 11–20. Continue doing this until you get to today; for Marion it was 55. You will probably find you remember less when you were very young, so focus on events such as starting school, the arrival of a new sibling, moving house, and so on. Write it all down.

3. Take the age that you are now, make that your start point, and then walk to the far end of your line – for example, 95. Imagine yourself at 95 looking back over the last 40 years. What have you been doing? How have you filled your time? Who have you been seeing? Where have you been? Where have you lived? Take a second look. Is there anything missing? Put in all the things you've ever wanted to do.

4. Now check out your list. Is it full of chores or full of fun? What are the things you've always wanted to do but not had the time? Make sure all of these are included, too. Do not just put what appears to be possible but also what you really want.

5. Go back to your line and walk from 55 to 95 through all those desires. Keep an eye on the list to make sure you have not missed anything out.

6. As you walk along the line, do any particular timings come to you – for example, I must move by the time I am 65, or I want a new job within a year? Again, jot down your dates. You will now have a broad overview of what you want to do.

7. Put your piece of paper away and let your head sort out the planning while you get on with other things. If any other ideas come to mind, then jot them down.

8. In a week or so, take a look at your list. It will be easy to dismiss half the ideas as not possible but that's going to limit you. Instead, imagine that there are no barriers, physical or emotional, and it is simply all down to your choice.

9. There may be things that no longer appeal to you – if that is the case, cross them out. Also, add in any last-minute ambitions.

First steps

You will now have started the process of creating the life you want. If, at any stage, negative thoughts re-occur, get out your line and re-create your dream. Before you move on to the next chapter, retrieve your answers to the questions posed in the Introduction and re-check your scores.

- Have they changed at all?
- If so, why? And if not, what's needed to change things?
- Having identified your dreams, I'm sure you will have new things to add to your list of what needs to be changed.
- What have you learnt that was useful? Highlight these or start a new list of useful things you've learnt.

Chapter Two
Managing Choices and Making Decisions

I ran a workshop recently for a group of eight people who were aged between 53 and 67, all but one of whom was working and most of them full-time. They were all feeling a bit fed up, not desperate but wanting to change some elements of their lives and wondering what to do next. They were also interested as to how they got to be where they are now – and whether that really mattered. Some had been in therapy where they had been encouraged to explore their past.

Knowing we're a bit fed up and doing something about it are two different things. If we want any aspect of our lives to change, we have to put in a bit of time and energy to allow this to happen. As a coach, my aim is to help you to identify which areas of your life you would like to change and to offer you ways to do this. I'm going to introduce you to some coaching ideas and techniques so that you can increase your repertoire when faced with choices and having to make difficult decisions. For many of us, understanding why we are, who we are, and how we got here is important, and as a generation we have been through quite a social revolution. Others of us are very happy to just start from now and look at ways forward. You will be able to identify your preference as you read through this chapter and undertake the exercises. By the time you're ready to read another chapter, you will be clear about which areas of your life you want to focus on to enable you to have a more fulfilled life – the one you want!

Social change

The course participants were all conscious that throughout their lives they had been faced with many more choices than their parents and many more than they had thought would be available when they were growing up. Without doubt, life had changed from the 1940s, 1950s, and 1960s when they were growing up. Two really significant things had happened in their childhood or teenage years. Compulsory conscription for men had ended in 1960 and any man born after 1942 was not called up. So none of the group had known the country at war except over the Falklands, which had not really affected their daily lives. The other significant social change had been the introduction in 1961 of a reliable, convenient oral contraceptive pill available on the National Health Service.

The pill

The pill was a godsend to British women, as not only was it the first time they could be in control of contraception but it also proved more reliable than anything previously available. Originally only prescribed to married women, the pill became widely available in 1967. This revolutionized many people's lives, and the ability to choose when you had children became commonplace.

How social change has affected us

Throughout this book, we will look at social changes and how these have affected us. These include changes in the workplace and communication, the ability for us all to travel widely, an increase in life expectancy (and the attendant increase in illnesses such as dementia), equalization in the roles of men and women, increases in divorce and step-parenting, 'boomerang' children, no fixed retirement age and its financial implications.

Early conditioning

Formative learning and conditioning in our families of origin shape the adults we become. War babies and early baby boomers were brought up in the 1950s and 1960s when the options and choices available were much more limited. I have often wondered over the years, when people are stuck and unable to decide between the options offered, whether part of their problem is that they have never learnt how to make decisions when faced with a variety of possibilities. Of course, it is never too late to learn and this is a good point to start. Coaching is a good way to explore what makes us tick.

My coaching approach

Let me tell you a bit about how I work as a coach. I trained originally as a counsellor and my knowledge and understanding of the therapeutic process underpins all my work. I later trained as a coach. I now call myself a coach-therapist. My aim is to help people to solve their problems and to create positive solutions. This often involves them understanding the inner conflicts, behaviour patterns, values, and beliefs that might be limiting their success. I also work with them to ensure that they meet their goals and aspirations and achieve positive results that enable them to have a more fulfilled life of high quality. To achieve this, you have to look at where you have come from with the aim of this helping you to get to where you want to be. The exercises I use with clients involve both processes. These exercises will enable you to have the life you want.

Clients come to see me because their lives have not turned out how they wanted. They have tried to make changes on their own or with the help of friends but are stuck and unable to make the shift. None of them feel old enough to stop dreaming and they want to achieve things; they all still have ambitions. They have questions about what they are doing with some parts of their lives and are wondering what they want to do in the future. I expect they are a bit like you, since you have chosen to read this book.

Our first course participants

I want to introduce you to six of the course participants, as I suspect the challenges they faced will be pretty familiar to you. Of course, they will not be the same, but there will be elements that overlap. You will meet other clients later in the book as we look at how they began to overcome their issues and have a more fulfilled life.

Michael, 63

Michael is 63 and has been divorced for two years. He'd married at 37 and had four children in the next eight years. He was a traditional man and saw himself as the breadwinner providing for his family and his wife who was the homemaker and main carer of the children. He thought he had a good enough marriage and was looking forward to a reasonably comfortable retirement in the future. Things didn't turn out as he expected. His wife went back into full-time work ten years ago when their youngest child was well established in primary school. She'd always worked but part-time and locally. Once she no longer felt she needed to be at home so much for the children, she got a job in the city and found herself increasingly bored with her married life. She met a new man and left Michael bruised, hurt, and unsure how to cope alone. He found splitting up the family possessions, including all their savings and his pension, very painful. He now lived alone in a much smaller house, and was lonely. He saw the children a bit but they were getting on with their own lives. He is a surveyor for the local authority and not unhappy at work, although he found it stressful at times. He had assumed he'd retire on his 65th birthday but now was very unsure how he was going to manage financially and whether he would ever be able to retire.

Bruce, 57

Bruce is 57 and a partner in a large international firm of solicitors. He's based in a UK regional office where he's been head of a department for a number of years. The firm, as it's a partnership, is still allowed to have a retirement age, which is 60. Their policy over the years has been to ask people to move on a few years before this to make room for new blood. The other less overt reason is that many of the older partners, although pretty good at their jobs, have not kept up with all the changes that have occurred in the workplace and are at times a bit slow. Bruce had just had his appraisal and, much to his surprise, his managing partner had suggested this might be the time to move on. He was in shock when we met, as he had no idea what to do, what that meant, and how it would affect him. He is married with teenage children and his wife doesn't have paid work. She is busily involved in local charities.

Susan, 62

Susan is 62 and was born in 1950 so had been able to retire at 60 from a managerial job in a local furniture store. She has a small work pension and her state pension. She lives on her own and has an elderly mother who lives nearby and has dementia. She has no children. She had never wanted children or to get married and it had never bothered her until now.

Retirement had caused her to think and although she wasn't lonely and she had lots of friends, she did worry about the future and felt she needed to make a new life for herself. Having worked all her adult life, she had some savings and, if her mother had not become ill, she could have pursued one of her dreams, which was to travel. She had hoped to apply to a charity and to work abroad for nine months and then travel for three months or so. She had fantasized about staying away for a while. She felt angry and trapped by her mother and felt that she couldn't leave her sister with this burden on her own as she had a husband and family to look after. She felt her life was slipping by and didn't know what to do.

Alison, 54

Alison is 54 and was in a very different position. She felt overwhelmed by all the people in her life. Seventeen years ago, she and her husband had wanted to move house but they couldn't afford it. Her parents who were in their late sixties at the time had suggested that they buy a place together. They would have the ground floor of a large house, while Alison and her husband and three children could live in the rest and they'd all share the garden. They would partition things off so they had their own space and this way Alison could move to the area she liked and her children could go to the local school. Seventeen years on, her mother has died and her father was now in his mid-eighties, unwell, demanding and needy, and her children (who in her view should have left) were still at home. One had a low-paid job and couldn't afford to move out, another had been to college and come home to pay off some debts, the eldest had moved in with his girlfriend but things hadn't worked out and he was back. Alison and her husband both worked full-time – she as a nurse and he as a manager in a large GP practice – and money seemed as much of a problem as it had been when the idea of sharing a house with her parents was first suggested. She felt overwhelmed and angry and that she'd lost her way.

Philip, 60

Philip, a web designer, is 60 and lives with his civil partner James. Half the week they live alone and the other half with James's 12-year-old son. James had fathered a child with a lesbian friend and they all three shared the parenting. James had always been in a less well-paid job than Philip and it had been agreed when their son was born that Philip would be the main earner and James would work part-time. He'd never envisaged that this would go on forever and, now the boy was 12, Philip was beginning to resent having to work so hard. He felt he needed to enhance his skills as he wanted to do something new with computers but couldn't afford to study unless James found different work. They also both had elderly parents who lived miles away and who needed increasing amounts of support. His other concern was that his father had died from a heart attack when he was 60 and his brother had died at 64, also from a heart attack. Philip had high blood pressure and cholesterol and he was understandably worried about his health and ensuring that his son would be provided for financially.

Pat, 64

Pat is 64 and now works as a PA to the director of a small jewellery chain. Her first husband left her for another woman when she was in her late thirties and it had taken her a while to get over this. She had three children to bring up. She'd always worked part-time in offices from when the children were small and had never imagined that she'd be in a full-time job. She thought she'd retire when she was 60, if not before. Her 'ex' had little to do with the children, although he had paid something towards their upbringing. As she'd divorced before the pension laws changed, Pat wasn't entitled to any of his pension and had very little of her own, as she had only been paying into a fund for a few years. Five years later, she re-married a widower with three teenage children and they bought a large house together. Her husband retired seven years ago from a good job but unfortunately his private pension was nowhere near what he'd expected. The step-sibling relationships were fraught to start with, then settled down for a while but had reared their head again as the children now had families of their own and were struggling and needed support. Two were in well-paid jobs and were doing fine. Of the other four, three needed some childcare support and four were struggling financially. Her husband did what he could to help with the children but Pat was busy all week although she did babysit at weekends. Pat and her husband were both really worried about their own financial future so felt torn between helping the children and themselves to be financially secure.

I would like you to take a few minutes to think about these people. It is time for the notebook again!

Ask yourself
- What did you think when you read these stories?
- Did they resonate with your life? In what way? Jot these down.
- Now imagine you'd been a member of this group and someone (with your permission) was going to write a brief scenario for others to read. What would be the salient points?
- Write your scenario of approximately 200 words.
- What are the issues that are affecting you at this minute?

Having heard from each of the people at the workshop, we moved into doing an initial exercise. I would like you to follow this yourself and then we will discuss it.

Making positive lasting changes

We only do something differently or better if we are committed to making a change. Recognizing and believing in the personal benefits will more than compensate for the discipline and effort required. To ensure we improve our performance, both in our professional and in our personal lives, we need time to prepare and plan. This involves asking ourselves the right questions in the right sequence.

The first exercise uses the premise that our brain focuses on the words that we say to ourselves in our head. So, for example, if I am very tired, I have two ways to talk about this. I might say, 'I don't want to be so tired' or, alternatively, 'I want to be energetic'. As soon as I think about being energetic, I have to do something very different like go for a walk or do some other exercise. If I focus on not being tired, I just lounge around on the sofa. If we want things to change, we have to look towards a solution rather than away from the problem.

Exercise: Focusing on the future

Part A

1. Read the scenario that you have written for yourself.

2. Identify which areas you would like to change.

3. Write down for each one what you would like instead. For example, Michael wrote: 'I don't want to be lonely.' I pointed out to him that he was still looking at 'lonely'. He

then wrote: 'I want to have someone to do things with' – a completely different focus. And a clear outcome.

4. Now write by each one of your difficulties the outcome you would like to achieve – what it will do for you so you're really clear why you want it.

5. Now look at your list and decide which one you want to prioritize. It does not mean that you cannot achieve them all, just in good time.

Let us now turn each of your desires into clear objectives – clear, precise forecasts of what you want to achieve in the future. An objective has certain known qualities. First, it has two parts to it: (i) a forecast of the aims to be achieved and (ii) indicators of success. Second, it must be realistic and possible to achieve in the allotted time span. Third, it should be challenging and pitched at a realistic level of achievement (and produce authentic feelings of satisfaction if you succeed). Finally, indicators of success are ways of measuring that the objective has been achieved.

Part B

1. Take your number one priority and follow the acronym SMARTER (Doran 1981) to create a good clear objective.[1] It stands for Specific, Measurable, Agreed, Realistic, Time-bound, Ethical/Exciting, Reviewed.

2. Before you start, let's use Michael's desire to 'have someone to do things with' as an example.

   • What did he mean by this? A friend to go places with? A lover? A live-in partner? There are numerous possibilities. He said after being questioned that he wanted to live with someone and share his life. That was now clear.

- Could he measure this? Clearly yes, as if someone had moved in, he would have achieved his goal!
- Has he agreed with himself he wants this? Again, clearly yes. Sometimes, we have to involve others if they are part of achieving the objective.
- Is it realistic? Yes, although a few actions are going to have to take place if he is going to make this a reality.
- Time-bound. He needed to decide on his time frame and meet a few smaller objectives first such as meeting someone, going on a date, and so on. This question helped him to break his goal down into manageable chunks.
- Ethical? As long as he did not coerce or exploit someone, it seemed all right.
- Exciting? Yes, just the thought had made him smile.
- Reviewed? He needed to decide review dates for each mini-objective in his action plan so he could see where he had got to and what, if anything, needed to be modified.

3. I suggest you follow SMARTER for the top three desires on your list. There's nothing wrong in discovering that your prioritization wasn't quite right or that two desires turned out to be pretty similar and can be run in tandem.

4. The final step is to develop an action plan (see Chapter 13 for details). This means determining the sequence of actions to be taken and the deadlines that need to be met to achieve the objective(s).

Well done, you are at the end! How are you feeling? If you are anything like my participants, pretty excited I guess. They all had things they wanted to do. What they still needed was help to see how to achieve some elements and you may be in exactly the same position. I suggest you now turn to the chapter that is most likely to give you the skills you need to achieve your priority dream. Once you have done that, see where you need to go for your next priority. Do not restrict yourself, as you might find there are areas that could do with a tweak, ones that you had not even considered. Whichever way you choose to go, end up at Chapter 13, as this will help you to focus your desires and enable them to happen.

So, if our six participants were deciding, what would they choose? I expect Bruce would go to Chapters 5 and 6 as he is interested in his career and possibly becoming an entrepreneur; Susan would go to Chapter 7 as she is interested in retirement; Pat and Alison to Chapter 9 to find out about surviving families; Philip to Chapter 11 as he is concerned about his health; and Michael to Chapter 10 as his objective is finding a partner. Which chapter are you going to read next?

Part II
Your Career

Chapter Three
Embracing Change in the Workplace

How did you feel reading the title of this chapter? Did you say, 'Yes, that's me! I love it!', or did you groan and say, 'No more! I hate change!' Managing change is essential for any of us living in the twenty-first century. Some of us do it well and others really struggle. Understanding how we approach change offers an opportunity to alter this and to make change work for us.

Managing change

This chapter will enable you to explore how you respond to change and provide an opportunity to adapt your style if it's not serving you very well. It will also look at the changes that have occurred in the workplace and why we've needed to be adaptable to learn new ways of working and communicating, as many of us did to get to the top of our professions.

I'd like you to meet Marcie, one of my clients. She was someone who really struggled to manage change at work.

Marcie, 59

Marcie, now 59, had left school with a couple of CSEs at 16 and started work in the typing pool of the local council. She was offered some training: she learnt shorthand and became a PA for a junior manager and later was promoted to work for a director. All was well until he retired. He was also 'old school' like her. He had happily dictated his letters, liking to see her with her notepad and she never had cause to complain. She progressed easily from a manual typewriter to an electric one and then to a word processor but the shift to a computer in the mid-1990s had taken some getting used to. She still struggled with some of the programs.

Her boss finally retired in 2002 and, since then, Marcie's life had been a misery. She found it really difficult to adapt to his replacement and left in 2004. She got a job in a medium-sized solicitors' practice, and struggled. No one talked to her, they sent emails even from the next desk, everything was on the Internet or intranet, and her boss sat next to her and used separate rooms for meetings. So she had no privacy. The noise was worse than the typing pool, she said. As they were an international firm, she was often expected to work late and, when she came in each morning, she was always behind, as there were already dozens of emails from the other side of the world.

The final straw came when she picked up her notepad to write down some dates for a series of meetings and her boss said, 'Why aren't you putting those into your Blackberry?' She could think of nothing better than the old days when pencil and paper worked just fine!

When she left, she thought she would 'temp', but things went from bad to worse. No one seemed to respect her even though she was years older than anyone else in the office. In one company, she had a boss who showed her no respect and was the same age as her son. It seemed to Marcie that she'd had to grapple with a new machine in every office and she'd had enough. She decided that, risky as it was, she'd have to set up her own business (as we'll see later).

Take out your notebook and answer the following questions.

Ask yourself
- What did you think when you read about Marcie?
- Does this resonate with you?
- Which bits did you empathize with and which bits made you cross?
- Are you a lover or hater of change?
- When it comes to change, what makes you feel the most uncomfortable?
- What helps you manage change well?

Marcie is not untypical of people who started work when the workplace was very different. It is easy to forget what it was like when we were starting out around 40 years ago. I have found it very useful when talking to people who are feeling a bit overwhelmed or finding it difficult to keep up to take a look at how far they've come. We have done really well!

Before we take a stroll down memory lane, pick up your notebook again.

- Jot down how things were when you started work; make a pen picture of it in your notebook.
- Make a list of all the things that have changed over the years in your experience.

Office life

Let us take a brief look at life in an office in the Western world from the 1960s (when some baby boomers started working) until the present day.[1] While you are reading, keep an eye on your notes. Add anything you have forgotten so you have got the complete picture.

1960s: Bosses and secretaries

The workplace was usually arranged so the managers and directors had their own offices. Men were the bosses and women typed. Men were always smartly dressed in a suit, shirt, and tie, which had been ironed by their wife or mother. The secretary wore short skirts and a blouse and called her boss 'Sir'. He called her by her first name.

The boss dictated letters to his secretary, which she took down in shorthand and then typed on a manual typewriter. Copies were made on carbon paper and the whole thing had to be re-typed if there was a mistake. The secretary's role was to meet her boss's needs, so, if he wanted a cup of tea (no coffee was drunk in those days), she'd be the one to make it. The boss would never make his own phone calls: his secretary would get in touch with the secretary of the person her boss wanted to talk to. When the person came on the line, she would buzz back and put them through.

Telephone calls came though the switchboard, operated by the receptionist who was always a woman. Her role was to greet anyone who came in, take all the calls, and type in between time. It was rare to phone abroad and those calls often had to be booked in advance. Employees had set working hours and one rarely stayed late.

1970s: Women's lib but not much change in the office

In the 1970s, women continued to type and answer the phone. Bosses were more often known as 'Mr' rather than 'Sir'. Although women's liberation had become a big issue politically, this seemed to have little effect on life in the office.

A huge change was decimalization in 1971, which made it so much easier for people using office machines.[2] Calculators started the decade as desktop machines. Photocopiers came down in price and were more widely available. Computers started to evolve and reduced in size while the mini-computer started to become the tool of choice, with large terminals starting to appear on people's desks by the end of the decade. Positions such as typists in the typing pool (invariably women), and junior level accountancy clerks, who were often men, were slowly being eroded. This meant many were made redundant and had to retrain in the new world of information technology. This has proved to be a very lucrative and ever-expanding field.

1980s: Office life relaxes

Office life was considerably more relaxed by the 1980s. People wore smart causal clothes, although men were still expected to wear ties. Suits were still worn for client meetings in many professions. By the end of the decade, most people, however senior, were called by their first name. Secretaries were almost always still female. There seemed to be a 'glass ceiling' that women met which stopped them getting to the top of their profession except in certain fields like teaching and nursing. More women were entering other professions such as law and accountancy, although few women made it to board level.

As the decade moved on, the typewriter gave way to the word processor and carbon copies were becoming extinct. In 1984, fax machines arrived on the scene and were fairly universal by the end of the decade.

The personal computer (PC) began its rise to prominence, becoming the machine of choice for all accountants. Desktop publishing became possible. Spreadsheets became a commonly used tool.

1990s: Work styles changed

Personal computers could be found in most offices but not on everyone's desk. New, increasingly small mobile phones and the Internet closely followed the rise of the PC.[3]

The full-time occupation of typist started to disappear and secretaries took on other administrative roles while men became administrators, too. Lunch was often eaten at the desk and staying late to meet international demands began to creep in. Women were beginning to find their place in both the boardroom and in management positions in medicine and the City, as lawyers and accountants. The first women to do this were mainly single women without children, as it was still virtually impossible to combine both roles. Their critics would say that they sublimated their femininity to be accepted in these roles. As the decade moved on this began to change and more mothers were reaching senior positions.

The world turned to email towards the end of the decade. The Internet was seen to have the potential to change lives but no one knew quite how.

Twenty-first century: The modern workplace

By 2000, office life was much more relaxed and informality began to creep into the clothes that people wore. Relationships between the boss and junior staff and secretaries were less hierarchical. Ties became optional in some businesses although most City firms – banks, accountancy, insurance, and property – still insisted on ties and suits.

The gender gap in occupations slowly began to reduce and it was accepted by most that both men and women could achieve great things. Systems came into place to assist women to have children without jeopardizing their career progression. It became possible for women to succeed to board level, although in some professions there was still little flexibility for women at the top. Many companies still saw working part-time as a death knell for a senior position and a career break was never as flexible as it sounded. We have continued to progress and we are now noticing a real shift in attitude and an increased flexibility in the workplace.

By 2000, Internet technology had advanced by leaps and bounds and the Internet was widely available in homes and in offices with the arrival of broadband speeding up the process. Computer screens became flat and light and freed up desk space. Flexi-time and job sharing were introduced allowing employees to work different hours to meet their other demands.

Everyone, everywhere had a mobile phone and 3G mobile phones became increasingly popular so emails could be picked up on the move with Internet access. Texts became the preferred way of communicating with friends, and emails are now the currency in offices with people speaking to each other less and less.

Visual conference calls are now commonplace and more meetings are happening virtually. Calling anywhere in the world is never given a second thought.

The changes we have lived through

The modern workplace has little resemblance to the one that most of us entered. It may have been a more rigid and traditional environment but we knew where we were; jobs were stable and a job for life was the norm. It was rare for anyone to change their career, unlike today when many have a 'portfolio career'.

Being available by email and text 24/7 is the order of the day and the boundaries of the working week have become blurred for many. People are increasingly expected to be available all of the time. Add to this social media, including Facebook, Twitter, and LinkedIn, and we are never out of communication with anyone for more than a minute or two unless we consciously turn one of our machines off. Today's fast-paced, ever-changing world has been a challenge for many of us. Coupled with this, the 'virtual world' has not stood still and every day there appears to be a new social media tool to learn (or, as some have decided, to avoid!). I have had to decide which of these new ways of communicating suit my work and my clients' needs rather than worrying that I am not using everything.

As the office hierarchy is less defined, we are all more able to participate in office life in an active way and have a say in the decisions that are being made. This brings with it some negatives – office politics! When decisions were made for us, we tended to accept what we were told. Nowadays, we rightly want to influence our environment and this can lead to different factions being created and sometimes manipulative and bullying behaviour, which for many can be difficult to manage. To cope with the new office politics, we've had to learn new interpersonal skills such as assertiveness so that we can stand up for ourselves when change isn't good for us and we wish our bosses to know our concerns.

Having read this history and identified the changes you have had to make, can you see a pattern in the areas that have caused you some difficulty? Make a note of these and use them when you are doing the exercises later in the book. You will be surprised how easy it is to shift these blocks. Let us now take a look at how these changes have affected our participants.

Unlike Marcie, many people have embraced the changes and are excited when new technology comes on to the market. Let us take a look at some of the participants we met in Chapter 2.

Susan, 62

Susan had done a lot of research into global communication, because she thought technology might be the key to her travelling as she could use it to talk to her mother on Skype. The challenge was getting her mother to use it! To this end, she would find a simple computer especially designed for the older person that is easier to use.

Philip, 60

Philip was now working in the new world as a web designer. He started in graphics many years before and said that computers had changed his world. The Internet had allowed him to move into a field he loved and to work in an industry that changed daily. He said he was a man who was easily bored. He loved the challenge of learning new programs, which, as discussed in Chapter 2, he was struggling to afford to do. He had an iPhone, iPad, and PC and was able to do things he had never believed were possible. Everything was so fast, he could get things done at a fraction of the time. He was looking forward to the next generation of phones and computers and hoped he would learn the necessary skills.

Pat, 64

Pat, on the other hand, had really struggled over the years with new technology. She said she has managed because she was interested and was willing to learn more but it didn't come naturally to her. She has watched many of her contemporaries fall by the wayside and leave high-powered jobs because they could not keep up. She talked a lot about her older sister who she worried about because she had failed to adapt to new software, had been asked to retire early, and had been depressed ever since.

Three very different responses to change! You will know how you would react from your answers to my earlier questions.

We all have preferred ways of behaving that we revert to automatically when faced with different sets of circumstances, and we all have a preferred way to manage change.

Complete the change questionnaire below devised by Rupert Eales-White.[4] This will help you understand yourself and your preferred way of managing change.

Exercise: My change preference style

1. Answer the 12 questions below. For each, there are four choices; choose the word with which you identify most. Score your first choice 4 marks, your second choice 3 marks, your third choice 2 marks, and the one with which you identify least 1 mark.

   Q1. Jobs – rank these in order of preference

	Marks	
Researcher	A	
Administrator	B	
Writer	C	
Social Worker	D	

Q2. Words – rank these in order of how you'd describe
yourself

	Marks		
Harmony	A		
Beauty	B		
Intellect	C		
Efficiency	D		

Q3. Words

	Marks		
Keep	A		
Evaluate	B		
Share	C		
Change	D		

Q4. Words

	Marks		
Idea	A		
Feeling	B		
Organization	C		
Fact	D		

Q5. Phrases – rank your behaviour

	Marks		
The right answer	A		
Safety first	B		
Go for it	C		
Sixth sense	D		

Q6. Sayings – which describes you most?

	Marks	
Smile and the whole world smiles with you	A	
Nothing ventured, nothing gained	B	
The facts speak for themselves	C	
Look before you leap	D	

Q7. How might someone who didn't know you well describe you?

	Marks	
Being a stick-in-the-mud	A	
Being as dry as dust	B	
Wearing your heart on you sleeve	C	
Having your head in the clouds	D	

Q8. Attitude to risk – do you prefer to:

	Marks	
Take risks?	A	
Share risks?	B	
Avoid risks?	C	
Analyse risks?	D	

Q9. Attitude to change – do you prefer to:

	Marks	
Analyse and evaluate ideas?	A	
Implement ideas that are practical?	B	
Generate ideas?	C	
Look to see how ideas will affect others?	D	

Q10. Actions you take – do you prefer to:

	Marks	
Make a new friend?	A	
Change your approach?	B	
Have a debate?	C	
Control a situation?	D	

Q11. How would you describe yourself?

	Marks	
Practical	A	
Rational	B	
Friendly	C	
Imaginative	D	

Q12. How might someone who didn't like you describe you?

	Marks	
Rebellious	A	
Weak	B	
Over-cautious	C	
Cold	D	

2. Score yourself using the sheet below. Transfer each mark into the appropriate column. When you have completed the form, add up your totals and fill in the scorecard.

3. Now plot your scores on the graph so that you can see each column in relation to the others.

Score sheet

Question	LD		CC		PF		PC	
1	A		B		D		C	
2	C		D		A		B	
3	B		A		C		D	
4	D		C		B		A	
5	A		B		D		C	
6	C		D		A		B	
7	B		A		C		D	
8	D		C		B		A	
9	A		B		D		C	
10	C		D		A		B	
11	B		A		C		D	
12	D		C		B		A	

TOTALS   ____ + ____ + ____ + ____ = 120

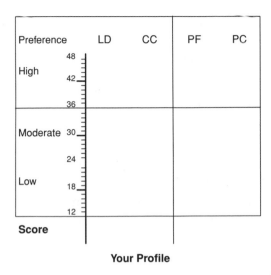

Your Profile

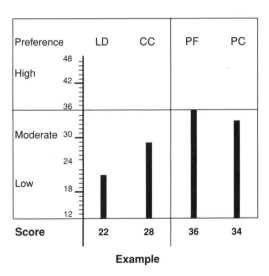

Example

The change questionnaire identifies four different ways of operating. It imagines the brain is divided into four sections (see below). Each division of the brain operates differently from the others (see Chapter 12 for an explanation about the way the brain works and how it affects our responses).

We can operate in four different ways:

- Think logically about the implications of change and be emotionally detached (LD).
- Think negatively about change, want to control it, and be emotionally affected (CC).
- Think about others, accept the change will happen, and be emotionally involved (PF).
- Think creatively and with excitement about the stage and be emotionally disconnected (PC).

See the diagram below for a pictorial representation.

Internal Focus	External Focus	
LD **Logical Detached** Analyse and Evaluate	**PC** **Positive Creative** Explore and Discover	**Intellectual**
Cautious Control **CC** Resist and stay in control	**People Focused** **PF** Accept and help others	**Emotional**
Left Brain	**Right Brain**	

4. Take a look at your results. Which one are you? Remember – none of us remains in one quadrant all of the time but we do all have a default position, the place we go to when uncertain, stressed or scared.

The **Logical Detached** person views change with an un-emotional and rational perspective. They are interested in the facts and the implications of the circumstances. Their focus is on analysing the situation rather than challenging the nature and dimension of the change or considering the emotional impact on themselves or others. On the positive side, they are careful, meticulous, logical, and analytical; they will have worked out the costs and benefits of new technology and its effect on themselves and their business. They will be keen to ensure that every new innovation is analysed, evaluated, and modified to meet the specification.

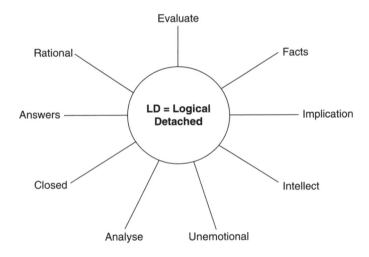

The **Cautious Control** person likes things as they are. They want to keep the status quo and their main interest is in how the change will affect them and those in a similar position. Their general standpoint is negative and they are willing to express their views with any argument that comes to mind. At times, they can appear to others to be illogical and very emotional. This person is completely unaware that they are seen like this, as they have a very different view of themselves, which in itself can hinder communication. On the positive side, in their resistance to change they are cautious and often able to help other, more impetuous people to reconsider before making mistakes. Once they can see the advantages of the change or realize that the change is going to happen in spite of their protestations, they use their organizational and practical skills to ensure that the change occurs in a planned, timely, and efficient manner.

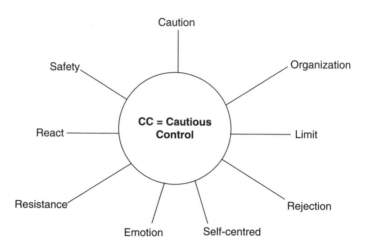

The **People Focused** person accepts change and does not appear to be affected by it personally. Their reactions are generally emotional; their focus is on others – colleagues and family members. They often speak for others and champion their cause, helping them to manage their situation. They like to communicate, so they often involve others and encourage everyone to share their experiences. On the positive side, they often help others to express their emotions so their arguments and concerns can be understood. The flipside is that they get stuck with their feelings – whether it is misery, happiness or anger – and find it difficult to see beyond this. If feelings are not discussed, they will find other ways of expressing themselves and this can manifest itself in inappropriate and manipulative behaviours, which can at times cause problems. The negative effect of this is that they often forget about themselves because they are so concerned about others. They can then end up feeling resentful and taking on the role of victim.

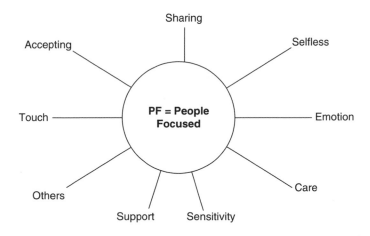

The **Positive Creative** person loves the idea of change. There is nothing they prefer! They get excited, want it to happen as soon as possible, and look forward to the challenges that change brings. They always look on the bright side of life and are always stimulated by new viewpoints. They get their energy from taking risks and having new adventures. The positives are: they are very future-oriented, big-picture, imaginative thinkers, who see multiple possibilities within any situation. They thrive on change rather than being scared by it. The downside is they do not focus on the emotional impact of the situation on themselves or others. When they have an idea, they can become single-minded and very demanding in order to meet their goals with little tolerance of other views.

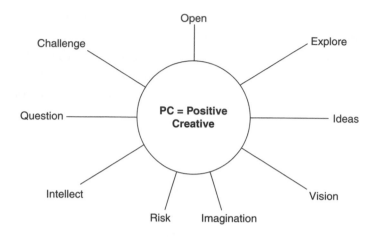

Managing others' change style

The pairs that find it the most difficult to manage change together are those who are diagonally opposite each other in the chart above. So, for example, the Positive Creative person thinks the Cautious Control person is always moaning even when they have not tried something out, forever worried about everything, and always harping on about the wonderful past and how the future will be awful.

The Cautious Control person believes the Positive Creative person is irresponsible and has no idea whether a new piece of software will revolutionize their working life but will anyway go ahead and buy it and ask everyone to use it just because it is new!

The Logical Detached person knows they are right: they have done their research, read all the reviews, met the manufacturer, looked at the budget, and worked out exactly how this new equipment is going to improve the balance sheet. That the People Focused person is worried about their colleagues and customers (and even the effect this will have on their family relationships as they will have to work late to learn the new programs) is enough to drive them mad. The Person Focused individual, meanwhile, thinks the Logical Detached person does not really care about anything but his or her profits.

Having completed the questionnaire and read the above, you will be able to identify where you are and what this means for you. You might also be interested to know how our case studies fared, which could help you to understand yourself.

Marcie is firmly embedded in the cautious control quadrant, while Philip is a positive and creative man. Susan is in the logical detached quadrant as she knew all the facts, and Pat is firmly in the person-centred corner.

So why is it helpful to know this? If we understand ourselves and why we do certain things, we have the option to do something different. We can question ourselves. Notepad time!

 Ask yourself
- Why am I feeling the way I do?
- Is this what I always do when faced with change?
- What else could I do? For example, imagine yourself in each quadrant and how you would behave.
- Make a note of the behaviours that would help you to move forward.
- Put them in action.

Modifying our responses

It also helps to understand others and why they are behaving in a certain way. Once you recognize that people behave as they do because they are worried, you can acknowledge their viewpoint even if their behaviour is very different from your own. Philip, for example, could help Marcie to see the positive side of our technological world and, if he was working with her, could help her overcome her difficulties. Susan could be helped by Pat to look at things from her mother's perspective, and that talking to someone on a computer isn't the same as having that person in the room. Susan, on the other hand, could explain the logic of why we have developed technologically as we have so Pat would feel less burdened with it.

This chapter has taken you back down memory lane to recall what it was like in the workplace when we first started out. It's so different from today that it's no wonder we sometimes find it tough. Now that you have an idea about your change preference and how to adjust your response, you should be able to manage your future more productively.

My top tips to manage the modern workplace

1. Understand that others have different change preference styles and modify your response to improve communication.
2. State your needs clearly so others can respond.
3. Ask for feedback when things aren't going well so that you know what the problem is and together you can work out a solution.
4. Offer feedback to others to improve relationships.
5. Be open, clear, and straight in your responses so you can avoid office politics.
6. Decide whether social media are for you and only learn about the bits you need.
7. Accept that other generations will use different means of communication.
8. Pace your working day and take appropriate breaks.
9. Learn to say no – no one can work 24/7!
10. Be proud of the fact that you're so adaptable and can fit in well in this new world of work.

Chapter Four
Being the Best I Can in the Workplace

In spite of the differences in the workplace explored in the last chapter, most baby boomers have adapted well to the challenges they have encountered and have been very successful in their chosen careers. They may be older but they are, without doubt, as bright and able as their younger colleagues. The problem is that many people in this age group don't believe they are. There are a number of reasons for this.

This chapter will explore the factors that influence how we view ourselves and the world around us, and how our own limiting beliefs can at times hamper us. It will look at our early educational experience and how it affects our thinking. We all go on learning whatever our age but sometimes we don't choose to do it in a way that fits our learning styles and our strengths. Understanding this will give you so many more options. And finally, we will discuss returning to the 'classroom' and the ways to do this.

Our education

All baby boomers were subjected to a fierce selection process at age 11, which decided their educational fate. There were three types of state-run secondary schools: grammar schools, which taught a highly academic curriculum with a focus on intellectual subjects, such as literature, classics, mathematics, science, languages and abstract thought; technical schools, which were for children who were adept in mechanical and practical scientific subjects; and secondary modern schools, where children were taught a wide range of subjects, including practical skills that would enable them to manage less skilled jobs and the home.

The intention had been that all three types of school would have a parity of esteem. This was far from the case. Failing the 11+ was seen as a sign that you were not clever and you were not going to achieve in life. Approximately 30 per cent of children went to grammar schools.[1] Very few technical schools were opened, due to the lack of money and a shortage of suitably qualified teachers. Consequently, the tripartite system quickly became two-tier: grammar schools for the academically gifted and secondary modern schools for the rest. In 1976, the Education Act forbade selection of pupils by ability and the tripartite system officially ended.[2]

Michele, 61

I met Michele five years ago. I was immediately impressed by her glamour and poise. She had come to see me because she wanted to think about succession planning for her very successful chain of clothes shops based in the southeast. She had no family who were interested in taking the business on so she had to look further afield. An extremely articulate and thoughtful woman, she had looked at a number of different ways to approach this.

In our second session, we started to focus on the type of person she was looking for to appoint as a manager. We decided to create a profile for the perfect individual (knowing she might need to compromise). Early into this process, she broke down in tears and said she couldn't have anyone like that as they would soon rumble she was stupid. When asked why she thought that, she said, 'Because I failed the 11+'.

Michele is not alone in thinking she is a failure because of this divisive exam.

Michael, one of our course participants (see p. 28), felt that one of the reasons his marriage had broken down was because, in spite of being a high flyer and getting to grammar school and university, he had never really used his education and was therefore a disappointment to his family and his wife. His confidence had been low throughout his working life and he felt he was increasingly left behind.

How do you feel about your own education? Time for the notebook!

Ask yourself

– What kind of schooling did you have?
– How has this affected your self-esteem and your career?
– Did you go to university or undertake a vocational career such as nursing or accountancy, or leave school and go straight to work?
– Did you feel good and empowered in school?
– How do you see your academic abilities? Would you have given the same answer when you were 15?
– Do you think you have succeeded because of or in spite of your schooling?

University wasn't for everyone

Going to grammar school was not a passport to university. Before the Second World War, only 2 per cent of 18-year-olds went to university. Now, over half of young people will have some form of higher education. In 1970–71, there were 621,000 students in higher education, a figure that had risen to 2.5 million by 2007–08.[3]

This is also true for secondary degrees; it is common now for people to have a Masters and some go on to do a PhD. These were rare when the baby boomers were younger. Many courses that people did attend as graduates offered diplomas and certificates, which are no longer seen as having much validity.

Michael, 63

Michael felt that he was always competing with someone who had more qualifications than him; even his young boss had a raft of letters after his name that dwarfed the few Michael had. He had avoided the training courses offered at work, as he was scared he wouldn't keep up. He knew rationally that he was doing himself no favours by missing out on the skills training, as it left him further behind, but his fear of being 'exposed' won every time.

Alison, 54

Alison (see Chapter 2) felt much the same. She had remained a staff nurse because she had never taken a degree. In her day, you could move through the ranks with her qualification but now you need a degree to become a sister or a community nurse. She had gone into nursing because she 'was not very clever' and even at 54 still carried round that label and felt trapped in her job.

Take out your notebook.

Ask yourself
- Do these stories resonate with your life?
- Are you someone who has held yourself back because you think you are not good enough?
- What stories do you tell yourself about your abilities?
- Make a list of all the things you have done at work where you have been successful. What could you say to yourself instead of the negative messages?

Philip, 60

Philip, on the other hand, had a very different story to tell. He had failed his 11+, gone to a secondary modern and, in his words, 'wasted his education on fags and stunts'. He had left school at 15, gone to work in the local factory, embarked on a relationship with a girl there which didn't work out (for more of his story see Chapter 2 and later chapters), and then moved to London and shared a flat with a guy who worked in an art shop who said there was a job going. While there, his boss noticed his 'doodles' and suggested he took up art. He went to night school, got the qualifications to study at art college, and has never looked back. He found it hard to understand why some of the others on our course felt 'stupid' and unsuccessful.

Limiting beliefs

In Chapter 1, we looked at how our beliefs affect us and how, if we believe we are stupid or less able than others or unable to learn, this will affect our ability to achieve.

Self-fulfilling prophecy

In 1948, sociologist Robert Merton described a phenomenon he called the self-fulfilling prophecy.[4] He used this to explain how a belief or expectation, whether correct or not, affects the outcome of a situation or the way a person (or group) will behave. In 1968, this work was followed up in the field of education by Robert Rosenthal and Lenore Jacobson.[5] They gave all the children in an elementary class in the USA a test, picked some of the papers at random, and told the teachers that these children were unusually clever when in fact they were the same as the rest. The researchers re-tested the class at the end of the year and no prizes for guessing who had done best. The children singled out had improved their scores far more than the others. This is known as the 'Pygmalion effect'.

I wonder how many of you are walking round proving these two theories? I expect most of you, in one area or another of your life. How often do you say to yourself, 'I am no good at X or Y?' Get out your notebook and make a list of the negative self-talk you have about your abilities.

For example, Michele said, 'I didn't go to grammar school and therefore I'm stupid, a failure and not academic'. I asked her when she had last undertaken an academic course. It turned out it was when she was 16! I then asked her how she knew she was still no good; of course, she could not answer me. I also asked her what she had been successful at. She was able to reframe her statement to say, 'I have achieved all I have without academic qualifications. I'm a very successful businesswoman.' She immediately felt better. Now do the same for yourself with all the items on your list.

If you are sitting in the workplace thinking you are not clever or not as able as your younger colleagues or that your qualifications are rubbish or that you will never keep up because you weren't on a computer by the time you were five, it is not going to help you. All you are doing is lowering your self-esteem. We will look at lack of self-esteem and confidence in Chapter 5, so you will feel able to ask your employer for the training you need to fulfil your role and to change your job if you so wish.

Learning styles

What I would like you to think about now is how you learn. If you know the way you learn best and you apply this strategy, you will find that you are successful 99 per cent of the time whatever you are trying to learn.

Neuro-linguistic programming

Let me introduce you to the psychological model of neuro-linguistic programming (NLP),[6] which was introduced in the early 1970s when a mathematician called Richard Bandler and linguist John Grinder asked themselves a simple but fascinating question: 'What is it that makes the difference between somebody who is merely competent at any given skill, and somebody who excels at the same skill?'

This simple question led them to create a model to understand how we perceive the world and how we organize our thinking, feeling, skills, and behaviour. It is a field that is continuously developing. NLP looks at what enables someone to achieve excellence and success. It is interested in what works and what works well.

My experience

Many years ago, I went on an NLP course run by Ian McDermott.[7] One of the areas we explored was how we learn.

It was only then that I became fully aware that we all have different ways of learning. If we understand how we learn and the blocks that limit our ability to learn, we can then make different choices and open up infinite possibilities. If we then approach anything new in this frame of mind, it will without doubt make the learning easier and the chance of success improves exponentially. The exercise below, which I learnt then, will help you to identify your learning style. Again, It is time for the notebook.

Exercise: How to identify your learning style

1. In your notebook, write down three things you remember learning – for example, learning to cycle, drive, swim, do an Excel spreadsheet.

2. Close your eyes and remember how you learnt the first one on your list.

3. Play a movie of the learning through your mind three times.

4. Repeat with the two other experiences of learning.

5. Now draw a storyboard depicting the strategies you used to learn the things on your list.

Step 1	Step 2	Step 3

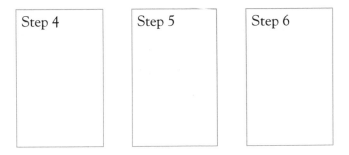

6. Take a look at your drawings and identify what helps you learn.

7. What have you learnt about your strategies and what causes blockages?

8. Now think of something you wanted to learn but have not yet achieved. Repeat the above exercise.

9. Now identify what it is that stopped you learning.

10. Are you now able to add the 'magic ingredient' so you can achieve that learning?

Over to you

Knowing your style is great but that isn't enough. You now have to use it.

 Ask yourself

— The final and most important question is: Now you know how you learn, how are you going to apply this knowledge?

— If you are at work, do you need to ask your boss to send you on some course or other?

(continued)

> – If you are trying to learn something away from work, are you approaching it in the right way? You might be in a position where you have to train others, so remember everyone has their own learning style. Teaching them in the way they learn will get the best results for both of you.

Strengths

Of course, knowing your learning style isn't the only tool that can help you. Alex Linley is the founding director of the Centre of Applied Positive Psychology (Capp).[8] He believes – rightly – that we're all naturally good at a number of things. It can be a skill such as time management or being adept at problem-solving or having the ability to empathize. If we 'play to our strengths' and use them, we'll be successful. If we ignore them, we'll find things more of a struggle. (See the Resources section at the end of the book.)

Many baby boomers have some years yet before they retire and will need to carry on working. I'm sure we all agree that it is really important that you are fulfilled by your work; otherwise, it will wear you down and become depressing.

If you find yourself either stuck at a certain level in your job, like Alison, or unable to move to the kind of job you would like because of your qualifications, it is never too late to do something about it and you will not be alone.

Active ageing

A comprehensive study, entitled 'Active ageing and universities: engaging older learners',[9] was published in 2010.

Its focus was the over-50s. Did you know that 60 per cent of undergraduates in the UK are over 21 and that around 40 per cent of higher education students do part-time or flexible courses? The 50+ made up 15 per cent of all first-year part-time undergraduates in 2007–08 and 10 per cent of first-year part-time postgraduates.

Returning to study

There are three main reasons why people over 50 study:

- to gain professional/vocational qualifications (sometimes supported by their employer);
- to attend non-vocational courses in adult and continuing education;
- to study for a degree but preferring a part-time route for financial, work-related or other reasons.

The top subjects for full-time students who are 50+ are education and allied medicine, with many looking for a career in teaching, nursing and associated medical fields. The next area of interest is the arts, humanities, and social sciences. For part-time students, the 'combined' category comes top, with students (for example, in continuing education) studying programmes across a range of subject categories. Many are interested in studying a language, which reflects this group's personal interests and preparation for lifestyle changes, as many hope to travel overseas when they retire.

It is good to know you won't be alone if you study, but how do you go about it? Take a look at the Resources section at the end of the book, which offers you places to go to get help, both in choosing a course and in finding funding.

My top tips for getting ahead

1. Let your early educational experience go so that it no longer affects you.
2. Remember that not having a degree doesn't mean you're less clever than people who have one.
3. Understand your learning style and let this guide you.
4. Identify your strengths and use them wherever you can.
5. Remember you're never too old to learn.

Chapter Five

Empowering Yourself to Change Your Career

It is my experience that many of my clients walk around believing that, because they are a certain age, they will not be able to achieve their goals. As we have discussed, this is a limiting belief. And, anyway, is it based on fact? Possibly. I am certainly not going to argue with others' experiences. What I will say, though, is believing you can achieve whatever you set your mind to opens up a whole new world.

This chapter will help you to think about your career and decide whether your grumbles are just part of everyday conversation (we all moan a bit at times about our jobs) or are serious fundamental issues. If they're the latter, you really need to consider changing your job or career if you're going to feel fulfilled. If you're a young baby boomer, you'll be in the workplace for approximately 18 more years, assuming you don't retire early, until you take your state pension. That's a long time to be unhappy. Many of us know we need to make a change but find ourselves frightened, as we have no idea whether we will be successful. At such times, we can be our own worst enemy and undermine our own confidence. I will offer you three exercises that show you how to improve your confidence, feel better about yourself, and believe sufficiently in your own abilities to empower you to change jobs.

This book is designed for both individuals and coaches to find ways to come to solutions for themselves or enable their clients to do so. I want to have a word with each of you separately here, as I expect you will have different aims and eventual goals.

For individuals, trying out the exercises, reading the case studies, and dipping into a session will enable you to gain some insight for yourself. You have already had some experience of this if you started reading at the beginning of the book.

If you are a coach, you will be aware that there are many different models of coaching on offer. Some coaches stick to one theory in which they have undertaken a rigorous training, while others will dip in and out of different models and theories depending on what they believe is best for their clients. I have introduced a model here that may be new to some of you. If you feel comfortable with it and it fits into your style of working, it is worth trying it out, perhaps with a colleague first before using it with a client.

Coaching sessions

We are now going to join two coaching sessions. My invitation to all readers is to answer the questions I asked both Marion and Michael and write down your answers. Even if my questions repeat, do the same for yourself and see what you come up with. I think you will be surprised. Of course, these questions could be applied to other topics but the one we are going to focus on here is changing career.

Marion's coaching session

We met Marion in Chapter 1. She had no real issues but felt fed up and was not sure why. I started the session using a technique called 'Time to Think'©, a technique created

by Nancy Kline.[1] She has developed the Thinking Environment and Partnership – her fundamental belief and building
block being 'that the quality of everything human beings do
depends on the thinking we do'. You will see as you read the
sessions that this elegant technique offers an opportunity for
the individual to think for themselves when they are offered
real 'attention, regard, and interest' by the listener. The
thinker will soon find they're able to think for themselves in
a very productive way, producing positive results.

The reason for this is that we often get caught up in trying to find a solution, believing someone else knows best, or
just reacting in the way we always have, listening to a critical
voice that repeats incessantly in our heads telling us we are
useless or incapable.

Marion, 59

I asked Marion the opening words of a thinking partnership
session where one person is the thinker and the other one the
listener: 'What do you want to think about', I asked, 'and what
are your thoughts?'

She replied, 'I know I said that I liked my job well enough;
the truth is I'm a bit fed up with it. Don't get me wrong. I could
do it for the next ten years but I just don't want to. The problem is I'm too old to change jobs. In my day, you were meant
to go into a job and stay there for forty years. I know people
don't do that any more but to start doing something completely different now would be mad at my age.'

I then asked her, 'What more do you think or feel or want
to say?'

She continued, 'I don't really know why I said all those
things. When I was younger, I never stayed in one job for
longer than two years. I believed I could pick and choose. I
wasn't the kind of woman who followed convention, much

to my mother's disgust. I just up and went. Somewhere along the line, I think I decided I needed to grow up, and that included staying in a job. Of course, when my husband and I split up, it was sensible to stay put, but we're through that now and now I can do whatever I want.'

I asked her again, 'What more do you think or feel or want to say?'

She replied, 'I don't know how I'd go about it. I haven't applied for a job in years and I don't know if I have what it takes or even know how to fill in an application form. What I need now is some practical information on how you go around this process.'

I repeated the same question.

And she said, 'I really need to think about what it is I want to achieve work-wise and how I could do that. Until I know what I want, I can't know if I can or can't get there. I also need to identify my skills so I know what I'm capable of. I'm going to write down my thoughts so I can work on this.'

We are going to leave Marion's conversation at this point and pick up with her a little later after we have looked at some of her identified goals.

Bruce's coaching session

One of our course participants, Bruce, who we met in Chapter 2, was very concerned about his career. He had imagined himself working in his solicitor's firm until he was 60, possibly coming back as a consultant and then finally retiring a few years later. It was a route many of his fellow partners had taken and he had not considered anything else. He felt as though the stuffing had been knocked out of him. He felt useless and hopeless and unable to see himself as anything but a failure.

Bruce, 57

I thought I'd use the same technique to start my session with Bruce. He clearly needed to think in a different way. I asked him 'what do you want to think about and what are your thoughts?'

He answered, 'How can I be a real man if I'm not a full-time solicitor in a prestigious firm? That's who I am, what I'm known for and what's expected of me. If I stop, I'll just be seen by others as a failure. How can I have boxed myself into a position where there's only one thing I can do?'

I then asked him, 'What more do you think or feel or want to say?'

He acknowledged that it was ridiculous to think he could only do one thing. For example, he said, he made a mean apple pie! What he meant was that he had become focused on being a lawyer and did not know how he could do any other job. He was not one hundred per cent sure how much he needed to earn or whether he could find something else to do that might be less well-paid but which fulfilled him. 'But who would want a man of my age? I'm 57. Surely I've scuppered my chances of doing anything different. What, if anything, do I bring to the table?'

I asked 'what more do you think or feel or want to say'.

'If I felt better about myself,' he said, 'then I could probably work out what to do. But because I feel so useless, every idea just goes round and round and comes back to a place of hopelessness.'

The elegance of engaged listening

Having read Marion's and Bruce's responses to my questions, please take some time to give this a go yourself. You can do it in one of two ways. One is simply to get out your notebook and ask yourself the following questions.

Ask yourself
– What do I want to think about and what are my thoughts?
– What more do I think or feel or want to say?

Say the words out loud and then ask yourself the next question. Or, if you can find someone who will listen to you, ask them to ask you the following questions:

- What do you want to think about and what are your thoughts?
- What more do you think or feel or want to say?

It is really important that the listener lets you talk for as long as you want without interruption and without commenting on what you say. Either way, like Marion, write down your thoughts afterwards so you can work on them later.

You may be asking yourselves why these two questions elicit this kind of response. The reason is that there is a true power in the listener's guaranteed non-interruptive, generative attention. They are asked with sincerity and interest, which allows the human mind to find and replace untrue limiting assumptions that the person has been living as true for years. Some of these assumptions are deep ones imposed by society, issues of prejudice and group identity, such as age.

I hope I have whetted your appetite to find out more about the Time to Think© and Thinking Environments®. Spare a moment to look at the Bibliography.

Opening possibilities

The conversations with Bruce and Marion raise a number of issues that are limiting their choices and have left them feeling stuck. Like them, I expect you, too, are reading this chapter because you have some interest in changing your job. This is a notebook moment! You may not have all the answers at this point but these questions will help you to explore your thinking.

Ask yourself
- How would you describe your working life?
- Which bits give you a buzz and which bits a sinking feeling?
- What factors are influencing your thoughts about changing your job?
- What beliefs do you have about your ability to get a job?
- Do you carry around a lot of negative thoughts – for example, 'I'm not skilled enough' or 'I don't have the right qualifications' or 'I'm too old'?
- What would you like to be doing?
- What do you think you need to be able to make a move?

Self-confidence

Believe in yourself. It is amazing how, as soon as you do, everything instantly becomes easier and more manageable.

Bruce clearly did not, so we undertook the following exercises, which I suggest you do, too. It is very easy when we are feeling anxious or worried or lacking in self-worth to forget that we ever had anything to offer. The next two exercises will help you to reconnect with your inner confidence and also help in solving today's problem.

Exercise: Building confidence

Think of a situation in which you felt totally self-confident. It does not need to be some grand event, just one where you knew you were doing well and you felt you could conquer the world. Now answer the following questions:

(a) What did that situation entail?
(b) What did you say to yourself in that situation?
(c) How did you feel?
(d) How did you behave as a consequence?

Now think of a current situation in which you experience a lack of self-worth – for example, looking for a new job – and ask yourself exactly the same questions.

(a) What does that situation entail?
(b) What do you say to yourself in that situation?
(c) How do you feel?
(d) How do you behave as a consequence?

Using your first answers, apply them to your current situation to see how you could change the way you feel.

(a) What could I say to myself that's positive?
(b) How might I feel differently?
(c) What direct action could I take – for example, to find out what's required for the new role I am interested in?

Exercises such as the one above are really good at helping you to think through a situation. However, just thinking is never quite enough. We also need to 'feel it' so we can know how to re-create that feeling within our bodies.

NLP technique

Now we are going to use a technique from neuro-linguistic programming (more on this in Chapter 6, where you will be helped to re-create good situations). This technique is especially good in helping us to change our mood when we are dealing with a difficult or taxing situation.

- Have you ever felt a bit fed up and then you heard a piece of music that reminded you of a wonderful occasion?
- As you think about that situation, imagine yourself there as though it were now. What happens physiologically to you during this process? My hunch is that you immediately feel happy and uplifted.
- Staying there, imagine the situation being even better – what happens now?
- Now imagine a new situation such as finding a different job. Keeping those positive feelings you have created, how do you feel? How possible does everything now seem?
- If you can keep that feeling with you when you are thinking about making a change, it will become more possible.

You can check it out by now focusing on one of your negative beliefs, such as 'I'm too old to get a new job'. What happens then? Yes, you feel bad! Every time you fall back into old patterns, try the exercise below, creating a circle of confidence, which is pretty much guaranteed to put you in a good frame of mind.

Exercise: Magic circle

1. Draw an imaginary circle on the floor in front of you. This is a magic circle. You can only be confident and excellent in here.

2. Stand outside the circle and think of a time when you were confident. When you have got it, step into the circle and take yourself back there as though it is happening now, and follow the steps below:

   – See what you see
   – Hear what you hear
   – Feel what you feel
   – Hold your body as you do when confident
   – Breathe as you breathe when feeling good
   – Really get that feeling

3. Now come out of your circle, stepping backwards. Think of a second time when you were really confident. When you have it, climb back into the circle and be there as it is now. Do this twice more so you can acquire confidence whenever you want.

4. Now think of something you have to do when you do not feel confident – for example, going to a new job interview. Climb into the circle and create that feeling of confidence:

   – See what you see going well – for example, the interviewer being impressed with your skills
   – Hear what you hear sounding good, such as you clearly selling your skills
   – Feel successful and bask in the knowledge that you can do this

5. When you have created these feelings and you are feeling really good, come out of the circle and walk into the 'interview'.

Repeat this as often as you can so this way of thinking becomes familiar. By changing how we feel, we change our physiology (see Chapter 12, where I discuss what happens within our bodies that enables us to create a new way of being).

The power of feeling good

I do not want to be unrealistic and say that just feeling good about yourself will get you an amazing job, since there are, of course, other factors. But what is true is that feeling good will get you a lot further and create more positive energy whatever you do.

For Bruce, just recognizing that he was good at many things and was confident in many areas of his life gave him the boost to begin to look at his future. Feeling confident and believing in your own self-worth is essential. It is also important to know what it is that we want to achieve. Marion and Bruce, like many of you, I expect, are unsure about what it is they want to achieve. One thing I can guarantee you, though, is that if you don't know what it is you want, you are very unlikely to get whatever it is. It may float past you if you are very lucky but the odds are probably the same as winning the lottery!

Take your note pad and try this exercise. It will give you a chance to focus on what you do want.

Exercise: Finding my work dream

You will need a little time on your own to do this. We are going to use a similar technique to the one you used in Chapter 1.

1. What age do you think you will be when you stop working? Include part-time work and voluntary work.

2. Now take yourself to the end of the room and imagine standing on a line that is your age today. Draw a second

imaginary line in front of you that represents five years beyond the age you thought of. So, if you thought you would stop at 65, the second line will represent age 70.

3. Now 'roll' that line up; we will come back to it later. Now draw a line from when you started work to today. See the line spanning a ten-year period and slowly walk up it remembering all the things you did at work, the skills you had when you started, the friends you made, your boss, and so on. Walk slowly up the line and, at the end of ten years, stop and jot down all your skills and attributes, all your pleasures at work, and all the bits that did not go so well.

4. Now do exactly the same for the next ten years. As you walk, you will see how your skills and experience increased. Capture all those points, including how you managed office politics, what made a good day, and what you found difficult at various points. Gather your skill and attribute set.

5. Walk along your line slowly, allowing your thoughts to flow freely. It does not matter how much or how little you recall. Take yourself up to today. Now spend some time focusing on your skills, expertise, attributes, ability to work in teams, to be a leader, and so on. At this point, I suggest you just jot them down; you can put them into categories later.

6. Now bring out your future line and lay it down. Take a look at the end so you know where you are going. Walk along it thinking about all the things you'd like to do work-wise in the future. Make sure you think of as many things as possible. Now sit down and record the things you want to achieve.

7. It may be to stay as you are because you have identified that work itself is good, or it may be that you want
a promotion or a real change or to work part-time or
not at all. You might want to do voluntary work or find
different activities or start your own business. All are
equally right if you have identified that they'll be good
for you.

8. Now walk along the line once more and check if
there were any goals you had that you have not
attained.

9. You will now have two sheets of paper – one with all the
skills, attributes, and experience you have and the other
with your targets for future work.

10. Now categorize the things you have written down by
separating them out so you have a column for each.

11. Having got this far, I suggest you put your pieces of paper
away and see what other ideas come to you while you are
getting on with your life. If anything else occurs to you,
jot them down for later.

12. In a week or so, take a look at your list – what do you
think? If your first reaction is, 'I can't do that' or 'That's
a mad idea' or 'I'm too old and no one wants me', stop
and take a look at your limiting beliefs (see Chapter 1
and critical voice in Chapter 6).

13. Your final step is to match your present skills, attributes,
and experience with your future desires. Ask yourself,
'Do I have what is needed for my dream job?' You may
need to do some research to find this out. One way
is to research job adverts for these roles and see what
they are asking for in the person specification and job

description. Another is to contact the professional body for that organization or talk to the company itself. You will find lots of information on the Internet.

Next steps

If you know your skills, you can look at job adverts and see if you can meet the requirements. If you do not have the requisite skills, find out where you can acquire them and enrol yourself on a course. Chapter 6 will help you to identify these skills.

Of course, there are practical things you need to do if you are looking for a job. If, like Marion, you haven't applied for a job for a while, you will need to familiarize yourself with electronic application forms, understand how a job description and person specification influence how you write your application and, of course, be prepared for a process that may include a presentation and more than one round of interviews, including a group interview. I am not going to explain these practical issues to you. There are many books and websites that can inform you on how to apply for a job. You can contact me for help, see the Resource section. What you should have now is clarity of goals and an understanding of what you need to achieve this.

Some of you may well have decided while doing this exercise that you don't want a formal job any more or that you want to set up your own business. We will look at this in Chapter 6. Naturally skills, attributes, and expertise are all essential ingredients when becoming an entrepreneur.

The most important point I'd like you to take from this chapter is that you can do whatever it is you want once you have identified your goal and you have the confidence to give it a go.

Chapter Six

Being Your Own Boss: Bringing Out the Entrepreneur Inside You

When we were brought up, it was unusual for anyone to start a new career or even a new job when they were in their fifties and sixties. You were either a businessperson who had started a business in your youth, or in a profession or job that you stayed in throughout your working life.

In this chapter, we are going to look at some of the factors that need to be considered when starting up your own business. We will focus on you as a person and your skills and look briefly at what you need to consider before you begin. There are a number of useful places to find that sort of information (see the Resources section and Bibliography at the end of the book).

New challenges

The way we manage our lives has changed, and it is not unusual for people to want to do something new when they are 50 or 60. The reality is you probably have a third of your life ahead of you, so there really is no reason why you should not take on new challenges, including starting your own business. Many over-50s do just this. It can happen for a number of reasons: being made redundant; feeling that, in spite of the Age Discrimination Act, you are being treated badly; finding it hard to get a new job; becoming fed up with not being your own boss; wanting more flexibility or a change in routine; discovering that your pension is just not big enough; or just wanting to run the business you have always thought about but the time was never quite right. For a lot of us, one of the plusses of getting older is that our family commitments have reduced so we have more time and more flexibility and perhaps a little more money.

Research

A number of organizations have done research into new businesses and those run by the 'olderpreneur'. The research shows that one in six businesses in the UK are started by the over-50s and they're responsible for bringing over £24 billion into the economy. Moreover, nearly half of the self-employed population is now aged over 50.[1]

Are you surprised by these statistics? A lot of us think we are past it and considered of little value to society. But that clearly is not the case. If this is how you feel, go back to Chapter 1 and look at changing negative beliefs (see p. 19). Another fact that may amaze you is that there are currently 2.8 million home businesses in the UK, contributing a combined £284 billion to the economy. Some 60 per cent of small businesses in the UK are started at home – there is no doubt that home-based businesses really work.[2]

Starting a business

Business start-ups by the over-50s have the best chance of achieving long-term success. This age group hasn't gathered all the knowledge, skills, and wisdom that come with getting older for nothing! The 50+ are also often the group who are more financially stable and have the most assets, so are able to fund the initial activities by themselves, although that is not true of everyone. Of the small businesses launched by the over-50s, 70 per cent are expected still to be trading after five years, which is much higher than the 28 per cent of businesses set up by younger entrepreneurs.[3]

An important point to make here is that I am talking about all types of business, whatever their size. Some of you could go on to create large multinationals but most will have small businesses that are run by yourselves or with one or two others. All businesses, of course, start from acorns, although some of the processes you may follow will be different depending on your goals.

Running your own show

In Chapter 3, we came across Marcie, who was totally fed up with life at work. She had decided the only thing left to her was to start her own business. A word of caution: if you feel similar to her, this is not a good starting point. Running your own business is hard work. There are none of the support services one takes for granted when working in an office – for example, an IT person to get you out of a fix when the computer plays up or the printer is jammed. You are often on your own and, unless you have a lot of money and can employ someone from the outset or have gone into partnership, it can be lonely. If all the jobs have to be done by you and you are going to put yourself on the map and be profitable, there's a lot to do. It takes hard work and it can be stressful.

To try and assess if Marcie's desire to become an entrepreneur was driven by her current situation or by a real desire to create a new business, however small, I asked her a few questions that I would like you to answer, too. Pick up your notebook so you are ready to jot down your answers. I want you to ignore the critical voice that whispers, 'I can't do that' or 'No one would be interested in what I have to offer' or 'I don't know enough'.

Ask yourself
- Find somewhere quiet to sit and start to daydream and imagine I have transported you to your new business in 2016.
- What is your purpose? What activities take place? Are you in partnership with anyone? You may even know what the business is called.
- When you picture it, what does it look like? Is it big/small, colourful, black and white, bright/dull, inviting/offputting, tidy/untidy? Is it in business premises or in your home?
- What does it feel like? Warm/cold, comfortable/tense, slow/fast, controlled/uncontrolled, happy/sad, high-energy/low-energy?
- How do people communicate? What kinds of conversation take place there? Open/closed, free/restricted, high/low, constant/erratic, pleasant/unpleasant?
- Who is present? Are you working on your own or with others? Are there people who come in and out rather than there all the time? Are there men/women/children – lots/a few? What types of people – active/passive, demanding/giving, needy/supportive, rigid/flexible?
- What problem or lack of resource does it meet in the marketplace?
- What is your unique niche?
- What do you do that no one else does? Why would I come to you?
- What have you been prepared to give up to make it work?
- What gives you a buzz and makes you smile when you think of the business?

Your business

How are you feeling about your new business idea now? Excited and raring to go, delighted you have got this great opportunity? You know you want to try something different, build something new, and spend time working on something you love. It will feel like fun rather than work when you are doing it (although there will be the odd moment when you have had enough). If you can answer 'yes' to all of the above, then it is right for you to pursue your dreams and see where you get.

If not, then your energy needs to be put into finding a new career as discussed in Chapter 5. Remember, it really is horses for courses. For some, setting up their own business with the uncertainty that goes with it is just too scary and thus is not right for them. Knowing what's right for you and following that instinct is essential if you are going to be successful.

Marcie's plan

After Marcie had answered my questions, she was ecstatic. She could see herself running an office agency that offered all the things she liked doing to companies who were outsourcing services. She knew from her experience in the job market that this was happening more and more. She also knew that in her area there were very few people doing it and it was a scarce resource. She was aware that if she were going to run a comprehensive service that met all business needs, there would be some tasks she did not particularly like doing. She was realistic enough to know that at the start she'd have to do these but after a bit she hoped to have a large enough client base that she could employ someone with different interests who would be fulfilled by different things. Marcie was clear that she had the skills needed to run this business. But she still felt she lacked the knowledge of what a start-up needed, which we will address later.

Bruce's dilemma

Bruce, who had been asked to leave his legal practice, was not at all sure what to do now he was not going to be at his old firm. He did not think starting a business was his thing until he answered the questions above. He surprised himself when he came up with the picture of running a sailing club for disadvantaged children in the reservoir near his home. His answers revealed he was very clear he did not want to be doing anything with the law. He had worked at a senior level and he knew he would feel demeaned if he were doing something in law or a related business that did not have similar status. He was very conscious that he had been fortunate and had earned a lot of money and wanted to give something back to the community. He loved sailing and he thought if he could combine the two that would be great.

For a moment, he was on a real high and then the doubts set in. He began to feel he did not have the necessary skills, so it was not worth thinking about any more; and, 'Anyway,' he added, 'I'm no good with children.' Before he could go any further, I stepped in, as it is very easy to get into a negative spiral. Once we are on the way down, we seem to slip and slide very quickly. We need to have strategies that stop us in our tracks and help us to think more positively. The other thing that surprised Bruce was that, although he had completed an exercise on his confidence and his skills earlier in our course (see Chapter 5), he immediately reverted to his habit of denigrating himself. I wonder whether you are doing the same thing and sending yourself into a negative spin?

Your inner critic

Before we look at identifying the skills you will need in your business, let us take a look at that critical voice. (You can also use the Emotional Freedom technique, which is described in Chapter 8 to clear these negative feelings.) We all have a critical voice. Some of us experience it as a constant refrain. I remember running a presentation skills course a number of years ago and my role was to provide feedback on the participants' performance so they could improve. One of the participants said she could not hear me because the voice in her head saying she was useless was so loud! Let us have a go at turning yours off. Pick up your notebook!

Exercise: Managing your critical voice

1. What are the kinds of thing you say to belittle yourself? For example, 'That won't work' or 'I'm not clever enough to do it' or 'No one will be interested.'

2. How often do you find yourself saying negative things – every second, every minute, hourly, daily, once a week, once a month? A lot of us find it is a constant refrain. If it is happening daily or more often, it is a habit you should be rid of!

3. When you say those things to yourself, do you hear the voice? Do you recognize it? Whose is it? Not everyone knows and that's just fine.

4. What makes you take that voice seriously?

5. Imagine a voice that you can't take seriously and makes you laugh, such as that of a comedian or a cartoon figure saying, 'That will never work' or 'Who do you think you are?' or 'That's a stupid idea.'

6. Change your voice to their voice – how seriously can you take it now?

I expect you will find you can't take it very seriously at all. Every time you get that voice in your head, change it to the 'silly' voice and you will no longer feel self-critical. Some of you, as well as hearing the voice, will also have a picture in your head of you failing or everything going wrong. If that is the case, you need to remove the picture. Try the techniques below. You will need your notebook for this.

Exercise: How to weaken your inner voice

1. Think of something that makes you feel good.

2. Associate into it – by that, I mean imagine it is happening now and you are there experiencing that special moment.

3. Conjure up five more thoughts like that.

4. Now join them all together so you have a mini-film that can only make you feel good.

5. Next time you get a negative thought, replace it with your positive film in which you are the star! Keep running it on a loop until you feel really good and the negative picture and the voice has gone.

Our brain

Our brain does not like to be empty. If we try and take a thought away, another will enter. Since many of us spend much of our time having negative thoughts about ourselves, those are the ones that are usually ready to jump in when we try to get rid of a thought. If you have your film reel ready, you can now replace it with the good picture and you will feel terrific. We will talk more about association and disassociation in Chapter 8.

Just to be clear: I am not talking about the voice of caution that says, for example, 'Is it wise to use all my savings and my house as collateral when I start up my business?' That is often a sensible voice and one that needs to be considered. It does not mean it is always right but it does need to be listened to and critically evaluated before being dismissed. Often, when we get a niggle that something just is not quite right, we are spot on. And, just to be on the safe side, take some external advice. So, in the case of finances, seek out a financial advisor.

Your skills

Let us go back to your skills. Like Bruce, you may be wondering if you have any! If you have not done the exercise in Chapter 5 'Finding my work dream' on p. 83 on skills, please go back to it and have a go. Now, it is time for that notebook again!

Exercise: Identify your skills

1. Write a list of all the things you can do – anything at all, in or out of work, big or small. You should have listed at least fifty things, if not a hundred. If you are struggling, first run through the last month and write down anything you have done and then ask others what they see as your skills.

2. Tick those things you enjoy doing. You may be very good at tidying cupboards but that is unlikely to be what you want to do as a new business. However, if you love it, there is probably a market for a professional de-clutterer!

3. Are your skills the right ones for the business ideas you had in the earlier exercise?

4. If not, are you really going to be prepared to work hard doing something you don't enjoy? Take a look at your business idea and see if you can modify it to incorporate the things you are good at and enjoy. Being an entrepreneur takes up a lot of time, so you need to know you will enjoy it; otherwise, it will be hard to keep up the pace.

5. Now identify which skills you already possess, which ones you could learn, and which ones will need someone else's help.

6. Do you know anyone with whom you could collaborate or who could be a mentor? The next step is to talk to them and see if they can help. If you do not know anyone, there's help at hand at a number of places. (See the Resources section later in this book.)

Having done the exercises, I'm sure you have identified that you have many, if not all, of the skills needed to set yourself up in a successful business. If you are still a bit unsure, identify where you can find some help and ask for it. The Resource section at the end of the book will offer you some avenues to pursue.

Bruce's next step

Bruce realized that he was without doubt passionate about his idea. He was thrilled he had come up with something that had never crossed his mind before. He identified the skills he had and those he did not have. He made a list of places he could go to and talk about the idea; this included his local sailing club and other boating clubs in his area, youth groups, and social services. He realized that if no one was interested, he'd have to modify his ideas. He also considered whether his idea might already have been put into practice by someone else. If that were the case, he had two questions. First, did they need another club and second, did he need to start one? Alternatively, he could go and work as a volunteer in an established club and offer to pay for certain pieces of equipment if he wanted to put some money into the project.

Check out volunteering

Volunteering is a very good way to know if you really like an idea or whether it was wonderful in your head but the reality is very different. One client of mine wanted to open a restaurant. All her friends said that she would find it too tiring and it would take too much of her time; she already had family commitments. She finally agreed to try it out before she took a lease on some premises. She contacted a few local restaurants and one said they would take her on as 'work experience' even though she was 51! She worked there for a month and realized she just could not do it at this point in her life. In the end, her solution was to go into partnership with three friends who were also keen to start a new venture. This way, they were all able to work fewer hours while benefiting from the new business.

Be confident in yourself

One of the most important attributes for success in any sphere of life and especially in setting up your own business is being confident in yourself. If you feel good about yourself, the rest will follow – I know that sounds simplistic, but it is true. A confident person who believes in their project, who has the energy and passion to work on it because they know it is good, who likes themselves and trusts their ability to succeed, is unlikely to go wrong.

That said, there are of course a few practical things to think about. Martin Zwelling's newsletter[4] is a good place to start, as he raises a lot of the issues and also points you in the right direction to find out more information. GOV.UK is another place where help is at hand, and PRIME, which is part of the Prince's Trust, advises people over 50 who want to set up in business.

To get the ball rolling, the following is a list of things it is important for you to consider, although it is by no means exhaustive.

My top tips

1. You will need a business plan – this is essential if you want to borrow any money and is good even if you do not, as it will enable you to see where you are going. Take some time on this as it will be the foundation of the project.
2. Like Bruce, check out the competition – there's no point starting something that is already available.
3. There are times when we think something is marvellous and everyone will want it, yet others have a very different view. It is always worth trying your ideas out on others before you go too far down the line.
4. If your ideas are considered worth pursuing, then create a dream team of advisors who can advise you with the activities you are less able to do. Everyone needs people to bounce ideas off. The first thing to do is

gather together a group of people whose opinion you value (this might include advisors from organizations such as GOV.UK), and tell them your ideas. All entrepreneurs have to work with other people – for example, partners, customers, and employees.

5. Decide whether you want to start from scratch or join a franchise. The advantage of a franchise is that the product has already shown itself to be successful, so there may well be less risk.

6. Are you someone who likes to work on his or her own and is good at taking decisions? Running your own business can be lonely, so make sure you have the right support around you.

7. Find a mentor who's good for you. They will need to be someone who's more experienced in business than you, sometimes in the same field, and who's genuinely interested in you and your business and who can give you advice and guidance. So as not to waste their time, make sure you know what you are looking for and keep them updated on your progress.

8. Remember that all businesses start small and grow gradually. Bear this in mind so that you don't become disappointed. If you set small goals as landmark steps, you will find it much easier to achieve things and be able to celebrate your successes. Celebrating successes is essential!

9. Find courses and people who can help you learn the skills you need – for example, accounting or IT skills.

10. Be willing to take intelligent risks.

11. Never be afraid to ask for help. The more open you are with others, the more you can learn. You need

(continued)

to be able to accept advice from others and even criticism at times and know that not everything will work. Being able to shoulder failure and setbacks is important. If something does not work, then see it as feedback, telling you what you need to do to succeed. Use it as a learning tool rather than a whip to make yourself feel bad.

12. Never assume you cannot learn something. The Internet is a fantastic tool for finding new knowledge and skills, so use it whenever you can.

13. Be prepared for it to take a lot of your time. You may have to give up your social life for a while so all your energy can go into this venture. That said, you do need to have some time off when you think about something else.

14. Keep your vision in mind all the time so you are clear everything you are doing will take you one step closer to your goal.

15. Enjoy yourself and have fun. Never forget that this is something you have started and that's pretty amazing. As I said earlier, if you have faith in your business, then others will certainly take an interest.

Chapter Seven
Making My Retirement Work for Me

Retirement is complicated. It raises both practical and emotional issues. We need to explore all aspects here so that you are free to make the choices that will enable you to enhance your life.

This chapter will focus on your inner relationship with retirement, how it affects you emotionally, and how to plan for your future. We will also look at money and how you can solve some of the problems you might encounter.

Contemplating retirement

When most people are considering retirement as a real option, they think about two things simultaneously: leaving work and being eligible for their state pension – and if they are fortunate enough to have one, a work and/or a private pension. Unfortunately, this is no longer a given.

First pensions

In 1948, a universal pension was introduced in Britain and there was a mandatory retirement age, most men retiring whether they liked it or not at 65 and women at 60. However, we are living in an ever-changing world. In 2006, a default retirement age was introduced which meant that workers could ask to continue to work after these ages. In 2011, the retirement age was abolished in the UK. This has received a mixed response. For some, it means they can continue working forever; for others, it means they are stuck in the workplace for even longer if they need the income. It has also opened up an element of choice, since it is now up to the individual to decide when they want to retire. For some, it was easier to be told!

Employers are also facing a new era. They will no longer be able to count the days until someone is legally required to retire. They will now have to find valid reasons to ask individuals to leave, based on their competence. This in itself is making many older workers anxious. They worry if, as they age, they will start to become less able to learn (see Chapter 4).

Modern pensions

Added to this, the retirement age or, rather, the age you can receive your pension, is now different. For men born before 6 December 1953, the current state pension age is 65. For women born after 5 April 1950 but before 6 December 1953, their state pension age is between 60 and 65. Under the Pensions Act 2011,[1] women's state pension age will increase more quickly to 65 between April 2016 and November 2018. From December 2018, the state pension age for both men and women will start to increase to reach 66 in October 2020. The government, meanwhile, is considering how to make sure the state pension age continues to keep pace with increases in life expectancy.

The effect on us

In Chapter 3, we looked at the social changes that have occurred over the last fifty years, of which there have been many. The change in statutory retirement age has had an enormous effect on those of us in this generation, in part, of course, because it is already affecting many of us. We may well have been planning to retire, only to discover we cannot or perhaps we do not want to and find ourselves having to reconsider our future. There are many who, even if they have reached the official retirement age, find they cannot afford to retire for many reasons. (To understand money further, see Chapter 8.)

I was talking to a client, Helen, who recently turned 60 and who cannot draw her pension until she is 62. She is someone who wants to go on working and is in a fortunate position, as she has no need to start drawing her pension now. Her job pays her well enough and leaving her pension untouched will mean that she will have a nice lump sum when the time comes. However, she still felt cheated by this change and that it was grossly unfair. For her, something has been taken away from her that was her right and expectation. She just could not get this out of her head, although she understood logically that as we are all living longer things have to change. After all, when the state pension age was introduced, many people did not live more than five years after retirement; now, it may well be thirty years or more. This feeling of unfairness was creeping into all aspects of her life and she wanted to do something about it.

Childhood influences

If this happens, it is often because it has sparked early memories of when you were treated unfairly or thought you had been, or something was taken away from you. If you did not find a way to resolve this, it remained lodged in your 'unconscious' and sat dormant waiting to be triggered. When something is unresolved it can resurface, leaving you feeling unsettled and uncertain.

I am sure you have been in a position where you have felt that things are not fair and that you have been denied something. Notebook moment!

 Ask yourself
- Think of a time when you felt you did not get what you wanted.
- Now think back to the first time you can remember ever feeling like that.
- What was the situation?
- What did you believe you should have got?
- How are you left feeling about it?
- How old were you at the time?

For most of us, the recollections are triggered by events that usually happened when we were aged seven or younger. At this age, we do not have the resources to deal with situations that we learn to better cope with as we get older. These old messages get lodged within us.

Our inner child

The exercise below will give you the opportunity to learn how to access your 'little girl or boy' with all the old hurts that sometimes get in the way and prevent you moving on with your life. The better resolved these hurts, the more able you will be to make the choices you need to move on.

Exercise: Removing old blocks

1. Find somewhere quiet where you won't be disturbed.

2. Think of an event when you were young and when you felt mistreated.

3. As you think about it, see if you can find the 'little girl or boy' lurking somewhere inside you. You may not get a picture, just a feeling.

4. Ask them as an adult what they needed as a child to have made them feel all right in that situation, much as a parent would ask a child why they felt bad about something.

5. Once they have told you, for example they needed someone to stand up for them, think of a time in your life when that has happened and share it with the little boy or girl inside so they know what it is like to have someone stand up for them.

6. Continue to ask them what they need and each time help them to meet that need. Keep asking the same question until they say they are done.

7. Now check out with them how they are feeling – I expect a whole lot better.

8. Suggest to them that, armed with these new resources, they imagine themselves growing up with all these needs met. They will be feeling cared for, even if things did not always go their way at the time.

9. 'Grow' yourself through your life until you reach the present day.

10. Now think about the unfair situation. How do you feel about it now?

Much like my client, you may not like it but you'll understand why and not feel emotionally overwrought by the pain and, that way, you'll be free to move on.

Expectations

The other thing that helped Helen move forward was a better understanding of her expectations. A common way of preventing us succeeding or feeling good about something is having unrealistic expectations. If we set ourselves goals or have a vision that is not achievable, we are going to be disappointed.

Imagine a scenario where you have been invited to spend the weekend with a friend who's moved away. You are really looking forward to some intimate time with them, catching up and enjoying their company. When you arrive, you find that they have invited some other friends as well. They are not your favourite people and what was going to be an informal weekend has completely changed. Your vision doesn't meet reality and you are disappointed even though the place is beautiful, the food is great, and the other people were all right in the end.

In a second scenario, imagine you have been invited to stay with some colleagues of your partner. She likes them and really wants to go but you find the friends pretty dull. As you have often dragged your partner to social events, you feel you ought to go but your expectation is that it will be boring and you'll be counting the minutes. They, too, have invited others and you instantly hit it off with one of the others.

After a couple of hours, you realize that you haven't stopped talking and laughing and you are having a good time. As the weekend progresses, you find yourself in interesting discussions with the host and hostess who you had previously thought were boring. As you leave, you hear yourself saying that this has been a great weekend and you hope to do it again soon! The event exceeded your expectations and you felt very good. It is all to do with Vision versus Reality:

- If the vision equals reality, V = R, we are doing okay.
- If the vision is less than reality, V < R, we are disappointed.
- If the vision is more than reality, V > R, we feel good.

When my client was able to change her expectations – or at least accept things had changed – she felt a whole lot better.

I said at the start of the chapter that we all react emotionally to the word retirement. Take out your notebook.

 Ask yourself
  – When you think of retirement, what images does it conjure up for you? It may be your own retirement or that of others.
  – How do you picture a retired person?
  – What do you see are the positives of being retired?
  – What are the negatives?
  – Is it something you look forward to or feel scared about? What are your reasons?

Make some notes to record what you are feeling or thinking now.

Imagine retirement

For most of us, retirement immediately conjures up old age and the thought of becoming less agile, energetic, and able. We often picture our grandparents who may well have been retired for twenty years and not just turned 65. We all know that retirement doesn't mean the end of the road but, if that is the picture we conjure up in our heads, it can be hard to shake off. If we can picture the future we would like, though, it will immediately energize us because it becomes exciting. All we then need to do is find a way to get there. Get your notebook out once again.

 Ask yourself

How would you like to spend your years between 65 and 75 and between 75 and 85? You may find it changes as you age. Add in as much detail as you can. It may well include working or doing voluntary work. You can use the time line exercise we discussed in Chapter 5 here but this time look at your non-working life rather than working life.

Retirement planning

Have you created the retirement you want? If not, go back and have another go. I am not asking you to make it realistic at this stage, just what it is you'd like to achieve. It never ceases to amaze me that, once we've set our sights on something, how often it is we achieve it. Not setting goals will certainly block us from realizing any goals.

Exercise: Retirement planning

1. Take your list of all the things that you want to do/achieve that you made when creating your ideal retirement plan.

2. Why are they important to you? Jot the reasons down beside them.

3. Prioritize them if you can; there may be a couple that are of equal importance.

4. Now write down how you will know you have achieved your goal. You may want to see more of your grandchildren, for instance. Be as specific as you can – seeing them once a month or having them come to stay three times a year.

5. The best way to achieve a goal is to have an end date so you know when you are aiming for; otherwise, your goals will shift and drift. Some goals, if you are not retired yet, will be difficult to pinpoint but try to narrow them down as best you can.

6. Now let us review that list. Imagine that a friend of yours has handed you the list. How realistic is it? If there are some things that are not possible at the moment – for example, buying a boat – you may want to modify this to renting one or you may want to change the time frame.

7. Next, take each goal separately and write down what it is you need to do to achieve it. So, for example, if you want to buy a boat, you may need to find some money. How will you do that? Write down all the possible ways and then look at how you'd go about it.

I imagine some of you are thinking this is a bit of a long process – but so is 35 years of retirement! I definitely think it warrants the effort.

Further thoughts

We started the chapter thinking about my client who wanted to continue working, and I'd like to go back to that thought before we end. Another occasion to pick up your notebook.

Ask yourself
- Now you can go on working as long as you like, why do you want to retire?
- Are you leaving because you worry others will think you are too old?
- Are you concerned that you might not be as able as you were at your job?
- Does your work feel like a chore or a hobby?
- Do you spend more time on it than you'd like to? Could you work in a different way?

Take some time to think through these questions. Some of the exercises already suggested in Chapters 3, 4, and 5 would help you to resolve these concerns.

Options

I would like to direct you to two thoughts. The first is that you do not have to retire. Some of us – often entrepreneurs but others, too – really enjoy what they are doing. It may not feel like work to them; it is, in fact, a positive pleasure.

I was talking to another client who had been unwell for a few months. He worked for a charity he had helped co-found more than twenty years previously. My client was surprised how much he actually missed the work itself. It wasn't the colleagues so much because he had been inundated with visitors at home. It was the work itself, the sense of doing something worthwhile. He became very clear he wouldn't be giving it up in a hurry.

Flexible working

An alternative that suits many people is to combine a bit of their retirement dream with a bit of work. These days, we are in the fortunate position where flexible working is now possible in many fields. This is another area to consider which you may not have thought of as an option.

So what is flexible working? It is any working pattern that can be created to meet your needs. It does of course also have to meet the needs of the organization; otherwise, even if they are legally obliged to agree to it, they will be unhappy.

Some of the most common variants on flexible working are:

- *Flexi-time*: choosing when to work (there's usually a core period during which you have to work).
- *Annualized hours*: your hours are worked out over a year, often as set shifts with you deciding when to work them.
- *Compressed hours*: working your agreed hours over fewer days.
- *Staggered hours*: different starting times, break and finishing times for employees in the same workplace.
- *Job sharing*: sharing a job designed for one person with someone else.
- *Homeworking*: working from home.
- *Part-time*: working less than the normal hours, perhaps by working fewer days per week.

Remember, this list is not exhaustive and there may be other forms of flexible working that are better suited to you and your employer.

Finding the right lifestyle

A clever way of meeting people's lifestyle needs that evolved with a team of designers with whom I was working was to match the lifestyles of young mothers and older workers. The mums wanted to work during school term time and the older workers wanted to work fewer hours so they could travel and do all the things on their retirement dream list. They decided to pair up and create their own style job share. Each pair was responsible for covering a job in whichever way they felt best. They each decided the hours they would do over the year (this way the employers knew what to pay them) and they then worked as flexibly as they wanted.

It's time for your notebook again.

Ask yourself

In what ways can you think of working flexibly, if that is what you want? Make a list and think about how you could achieve this.

Take the challenge

I think as a generation we have been remarkably lucky. We have been given so many opportunities to do things in our own way. The rigid rules our grandparents and parents had to follow no longer apply. The downside of course is we have to make decisions and decide what is best for us. Retirement is a good example; we can choose if or when we retire. It is really important that each and every one of us works out what is best for both ourselves and our families and that we pursue a goal that will fulfil our lives.

Part III
Your Lifestyle

Chapter Eight
Money, money, money

Thinking back to your childhood, where did you imagine you would be at this stage in your life? I expect with everything all sorted out, including your finances. But, for many of us, this is not the case. If you find yourself fed up and feeling life is not fair, you're probably suffering from 'Vision doesn't equal Reality' as discussed in Chapter 7. Being realistic about where you are is essential unless you want to carry on being miserable.

I wonder how many of you are feeling bad about money and share some of the emotions mentioned – shame, fear, guilt? This chapter will focus on helping you manage your feelings about money while also touching on the practical aspects. Please take a look at the Resources section at the end of the book for good advice and places to go.

The economic climate

There could be many reasons why things are not as you expected. For some, it is because the world has changed. No one predicted the collapse of the banks in 2007–08, or the UK going into recession in January 2009. Whatever your finances, you will have been affected.

Pension provision

Final pensions are no longer a given; private pensions for many will fall short of the original projections; endowment policies taken on mortgages have been squeezed; university fees have gone through the roof; children are unable to cover the costs of living independently; and so on. Coupled with this, the increase in the number of divorces in this generation means that many people are once again single and running their own homes while some are also making maintenance payments.

Divorce

Divorcees have an added problem with their pensions. Before 1999, the partner with a pension did not have to give their spouse any of it. Since 1999 for marriages and 2004 for civil partnerships, the partner with the higher pension settlement is required to give a proportion of their pension to their ex-partner.

Married women

Married women in their forties and fifties may still be paying what is called the 'reduced rate' married woman's National Insurance contributions. These contributions were abolished for women who first started contributing after April 1977. More than a million women under 60 have paid them at some time and many more who are older. The reduced rate earns you, in effect, nothing. You get no rights to a retirement pension, no rights to Jobseeker's Allowance, and no rights to sickness benefit. This has left some women in a very difficult position. Getting advice on this from a financial advisor is important, as past contributions may be able to be paid back.

Sobering facts

An ICM poll undertaken in 2012 for Age UK found that over half of the people over 60 interviewed were finding it more difficult to live on their incomes than a year previously.[1] Nine per cent of people over 60 surveyed said that they were finding it quite difficult or even struggling to manage on their income, with a third only able to afford 'the basics'. The study also showed that this group are cutting back on fuel and energy for heating, with 14 per cent of over-60s saying they have gone to bed early in order to keep warm, and 13 per cent living in one room to save money on heating.

Money worries

Not surprisingly, one of the topics that resonated with all the participants on my course who you met in Chapter 2 was money. Most said worrying about money was what kept them awake at night. They were anxious about their future and ending up in 'the poor house'. Take Michael – he is divorced and worrying how he can make ends meet. I want to share with you a conversation he had with us.

Michael, 63

'I'm finding it extremely hard to talk to you about this as I feel so ashamed. I'm 63 and I don't have enough money to manage. Any decent man who provided well for his family should be able to do so till their dying days and also be able to help their children get established in their own homes. My youngest child is going to university this year and I have another in the third year. I have no idea how I'll cope with the fees. When we had the kids, we never dreamt we'd be paying out £9000 a year for their further education. My eldest two are living in rented flats and really want to buy. I can't give them any money for a deposit so they're stuck. My ex-wife will of course help but she doesn't have much, either. I'm filled with fear about the future and what it will bring. I know I'm only going to get older and have less energy and be less able to provide for myself. Eventually, I'll need care. How will I manage without money? I know I'm not there yet but it's these thoughts that keep me awake at night. I know deep down that there are things I can do but that doesn't stop the shame and fear.'

Susan, 62

Susan chipped in. 'I spend most days worrying about money. Although I have a good enough pension, it is not going to allow me to do the things I want to do. It's so tedious having to think about money all the time. I've got friends who are married and seem to have lots of money; some even have two houses and it is not an issue for them. I sometimes find myself consumed with envy, which is not a great feeling.'

Sarah, 59

Let me introduce you to Sarah, another participant who is 59 and has worked all her life. Her husband is an artist and has never been very successful at selling his paintings. He works as an art teacher at a couple of evening classes but he has never brought in the family income. She ran her own business for a while but it never really recovered from the early 1990s recession and, by the late 1990s, she decided to shut up shop. She is a designer and people just weren't using interior designers in the way they had done before. She applied for a position in a related industry and was amazed that at 48 they offered her a job. She had 11 good years there and then 8 months ago was made redundant. She is struggling to find work and is toying with re-starting her own business but the economic climate is just not right. She, like Michael, is ashamed that she is in this position. Scared about the future, like Susan she is envious of others. She kept repeating over and over again that it was not meant to be like this.

Alison, 54

Alison joined in: 'My fear, like Michael's, is about managing my family and helping them on their way. My children are still at home and I can't see them ever moving out. We can't afford to have them with us and we can't afford to help them to buy somewhere for themselves. I feel so guilty as we really did take time to plan our lives, working out our finances and commitments hence finding a house for all the family. Now we're here, it just is not where I hoped to be.'

Pat, 64

Finally, Pat had her say. 'I've been sitting here listening to you all talk and, although it doesn't help my situation one bit, I feel so much better that I'm not alone. I thought everyone else had it right! I keep telling my husband that, by this age, we should have been able to do X and Y. I'm sorry you're all in a similar position because I know it's not nice. I wonder why it is we don't talk about it more. As Michael said, it's probably because we're ashamed; silly really as it doesn't help to bottle things up.'

The other four agreed with her and said that it was a relief to get this off their chest. They spent their lives pretending to people that everything was all right. They had nowhere to go with their problems. It felt impossible to share them because they worried they would be pitied and that was the last thing they needed.

Sharing our concerns

I have to say I disagree with them: we all know someone who will listen to us. Talking about our problems to others is really important; in fact, I would go so far as to say essential. Sometimes, as we saw earlier with Marion and Bruce in Chapter 5, just talking out loud with no verbal input from anyone else can create solutions. Often, it is helpful to share whatever it is with someone else – a friend who can listen and on occasion offer advice, or a professional who can help you find your own solutions or an advisor who knows more about the subject. However, it needs to have a purpose. I am advocating talking because you want to look for a solution, not moaning because you want to get it off your chest and leave the other person with the problem! I am sure we have all done it at times but it is not productive.

Bruce, 57

Bruce, whom we know had earned well, remained quiet throughout this discussion. He said he felt very guilty having listened, as this was not what kept him awake at night. Like many, he was not as well off as he had been because of a change in the value of his investments. This was not a problem for him as he had no debts and was able to manage his outgoings. He knew people who appeared very wealthy but had outgoings they could no longer manage and assets they couldn't sell. He said it was the luck of the draw that he had gone into a job that paid so well; some of the alternatives wouldn't have paid so well. One of his reasons for wanting to do something like set up a sailing school was to give something to those who needed it most.

Many of us spend a lot of our time, like Michael, worrying about things in the future that we really do not need to. Of course, we do not know that at the time. We create a picture in our heads and then, because it is there, believe it is right.

Your future financial situation

Let us try something out. It is a notebook moment. Imagine yourself and your finances in 10 years' time. Scroll forward and create a picture so you can see life as it is then.

Ask yourself
- What is your financial situation?
- Are you able to do everything you want?
- Are you worrying about money?
- Are you still working because you can't afford to retire?
- What are the conversations you are having with people concerning money?
- If you have children, are they well established or do you worry about their financial situation?

Now come away from that picture and answer the following questions. When you were thinking about yourself and your future were you:
- inside your body, looking out through your eyes?
- in the moment, as though it was real time?
- aware of bodily sensations and feelings?
- actively engaging in the conversation, hearing everyone's voices, and being aware of the variety in tone and tempo?

If the answer to any of the above was 'yes', you were associated into the event and living it as if it were real and happening now.

Or was any of the following your experience:
- outside your body, observing the scenario?
- watching the action unfold?
- no awareness of bodily sensations and feelings; only your own as an observer?
- knowing a conversation was going on that you were listening to but not hearing your own voice?

If so, you were disassociated from the event as though you were seeing yourself from a different place. It was a scene you were in and not something happening now.

Anxiety

Several of our participants reported that they were kept awake worrying and feeling the anxiety as though it were happening now. When that occurs, we have associated into our future and are living whatever misery it is that has befallen us as though it is occurring now. We become overwhelmed with emotion and spiral down into what can feel like a very deep well with no way out. What we need to do is convince ourselves this is not happening now and step out of the picture. As soon as you do, you can then begin to make a decision about how to deal with what's happening from a rational standpoint. When associated, we're full of fear, and fear paralyses. We become the rabbit in the headlight.

Getting advice

You may be right about your finances and you may be heading for major financial problems that cannot be averted but more than likely you will be all right. You may need to make a few changes but that's very different from not being able to pay your way. One way to get a proper overview of your finances is to talk to a financial advisor. Most of us do not have the knowledge needed to plan our finances but financial advisors have specialist knowledge and understand the financial services market. They can help you to identify your priorities and put together a plan to help you to achieve them. Some will charge for doing this and others will earn their fee from the financial products you buy. Of course, you can try doing this yourself but it will take a while and you might overlook something.

Taking action

Worrying about money and feeling really negative about it is not going to improve your finances. The best way to help yourself is to dispel those negative feelings and immediately you will feel more resourceful.

I am now going to introduce you to a technique that can help you manage negative feelings. The example we're going to use is related to money. If this does not fit for you, think of something it would work for and use that instead. For instance, lack of confidence is a good substitute.

Emotional Freedom Technique

The Emotional Freedom Technique (EFT)[2] is based on the idea that we have energy flowing through our body, which gets blocked when we have negative thoughts and feelings. If we can balance the natural flow of the body's energy system, we will feel better. If you have ever had a 'bad hair day', you will know that your body contains a great deal of energy. When that energy flows smoothly, we feel good; when it gets blocked, we feel low. EFT has its routes in ancient Chinese medicine. It works through stimulating the energy meridians (as used in acupuncture), a network of pathways that traverse the body and through which invisible energy flows.

EFT is a non-needle version of acupuncture. By tapping on the ends of meridian points, it is possible to move energy along and help it flow through the body. The fundamental belief behind EFT, in the words of its founder Gary Craig, is that: 'The cause of all negative emotions is a disruption in the body's energy system,' and that, while these remain unresolved, they can cause physical and emotional pain and illness.

Craig's lifelong interest in personal improvement psychology led him to the field of energy therapy. In the 1920s, Albert Einstein stated that everything (including our bodies) is composed of energy. Craig studied with Roger Callahan, a clinical psychologist who discovered that stimulating the acupressure points by touch enabled his patients to deal with and dispel long-held phobias. Callahan explored through his therapeutic work the energy factors behind the common conflict that we have between wanting to change something and our resistance to that change. Gary Craig has built on this and produced a clear and simple formula that has remarkable success rates.

Removing our blocks

Our concerns about money can cause blockages in our energy system – this is a bit like a break in the Christmas tree lights' electrical circuit – and a negative emotion is set up. If it is a severe break in our body's energy flow, the system stops working and we can end up physically sick or emotionally out of sorts. If it is less severe, it goes on working like the lights: they're all right if you don't touch them but they remain unpredictable unless the root problem is addressed.

EFT has a very clear, easy-to-learn routine, which combines articulating the problem with tapping. So you can do it yourself at home. Please note that no EFT practitioner would claim that it replaces medical treatment for physical or mental health problems. When trying it on yourself, you should be as careful as you would be if you were practising a yoga handstand at home or swimming in a pool without a lifeguard – so stay in the shallow end!

Let's now go through the basic steps so you can tap on your negative feelings. I am going to use Michael as our demonstration model.

Exercise: Creating positive feelings

1. Start by thinking of the problem and rating the intensity on a scale from 0 to 10 (0 being least intense and 10 being most intense). Michael gave his fear about money a 10.

2. Before tapping, you need to create a statement about your problem. This is called the set-up statement and is composed of two parts: it clearly states the problem and then adds a positive affirmation, such as 'I completely accept myself'. This helps put your body into a receptive state and stops you adding all the negative bits – for example, if you were to say, 'I will now feel good about money', you won't immediately add, 'No, I won't because of x, y and z.' This two-part process is known as psychological reversal and it stops your unconscious working against your conscious mind.

3. Take a look at the figures below and get ready to tap. You can use either hand and you tap by using your index and middle fingers.

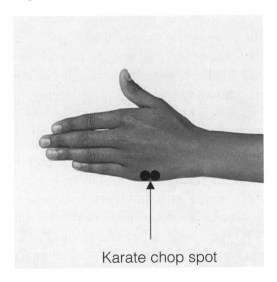

Karate chop spot

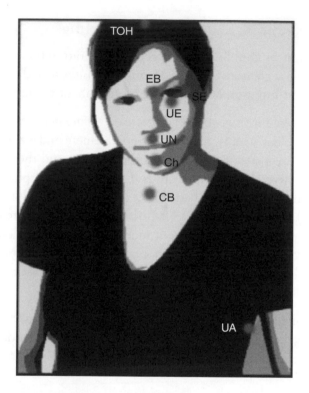

4. Start by tapping the 'Karate Chop' point continuously (see the figure on p. 125)[3] and say your 'set-up statement' out loud. Michael's was: 'Even though I'm worried about money now and when I think about ageing, I completely love and accept myself.'

5. You then tap each acupressure point (see the figure above) up to seven times while repeating some part of the negative bit of the statement – in Michael's case, 'I feel worried about money now and when I think about ageing.' The sequence is: end of eyebrow, near nose; side of eye, on bone (in other words, other end of eyebrow); under eye; under nose; under mouth (chin); collarbone; under arm; and top of head.

Here is what Michael said on tapping those places:

- Eyebrow: 'I'm worried about money.'
- Side of eye: 'I do not have enough money.'
- Under eye: 'I do not want to be poor when I'm old.'
- Under nose: 'I do not want to age.'
- Under mouth: 'I feel scared I won't be able to manage my life.'
- Collarbone: 'Money is a worry.'
- Under arm: 'I do not want my children to suffer from my lack of money.'
- Top of head: 'I'm sorry I do not have enough money.'

6. Then tap, stating what you would prefer, rather than what you are continually experiencing. This allows you to introduce the positive into the system.

So Michael said:

- Eyebrow: 'I feel good about how I've managed my money so far.'
- Side of eye: 'I like the fact my family has not gone without.'
- Under eye: 'I appreciate how well I've done to send my children to university.'
- Under nose: 'I have let go of the fear of being poor.'
- Under mouth: 'I like the house I live in and pay for.'
- Collarbone: 'I know I am resourceful and can find ways of making money.'
- Under arm: 'I am a planner so can plan for my old age.'
- Top of head: 'I enjoy knowing my children have the skills to develop their own lives.'

Now take a deep breath and go back and think of worrying about money in the middle of the night. Ask yourself if you would still score 10 points – or somewhere lower. Unless you went to zero, continue tapping for several rounds but this time start the round with: 'Even though I still have feelings about lack of money now and when I'm older.' This way, you will acknowledge that the negative feeling remains but it is now different from how it was. And see what happens.

Try something new

Even though the idea of tapping on acupressure points sounds odd and unlikely, and you may not believe it can be of any use, give it a go! If you find it helps, do it again; if not, move on to something else. There is some information on EFT in the Resources section at the end of the book, and a wealth of information on the Internet. Sometimes, if the problem is resistant, it can be helpful to find an experienced practitioner to work with you on your negative issues. One of the things I have found for myself as well as my clients is that a combination of both works well. Using a professional and then continuing the tapping on a daily basis between sessions really does help get results.

I know that it is much easier to manage your life comfortably if you have enough money. I am reminded of a client who came to see me after her husband's business had failed. She was angry and found herself caught up in this rather than looking at how she could manage. Once she had begun to focus on this, we looked at how she could still do things and have a good time without spending much money. We brainstormed ideas about what could be done for free or little money and her homework was to come back with a list of at least ten things. The Internet is a wonderful source of information.

It is very easy to let our fears and anxieties about money run away with us. Learning how to feel positive about what we have and appreciate it is really important and will lead to a happy and positive life.

Coping on little money

It's very easy to allow your worries about money to over-whelm you and leave you in an unproductive place where you go round and round in circles rather than finding a solution. If you use some of the ideas in this chapter, you will find that you are able to both create your own solutions and find others to help you. One last thing to do before I give you a few tips on things you can do on a small budget is to take that notebook and make a list of the things you think you can do on next to nothing. See if you can list ten. The Resource section at the end of the book lists sites you can go to for information.

My top tips

1. Apply to see films before they're out for free (see Resources section).
2. Apply to see radio and TV programmes for free when they're recorded.
3. Borrow an audio kit from your local library and learn a new language.
4. Visit free festivals and community events.
5. Volunteer locally or for a foreign holiday (see website in Resources section).
6. Sell what you do not need at car boot sales and via eBay.
7. Join a book club.
8. Arrange dinners at friends' houses rather than eating out and agree a small budget that can be spent by the hosts.
9. Only buy things that are on special offer – check out all the voucher sites.
10. Plant a vegetable patch and grow your own food, or see if someone at your local allotment would like help in exchange for home-grown produce.

Chapter Nine
Families and How to
Survive Them

Ask anyone about their family and they have a lot to say! More than anything else, families cause our emotions to fluctuate. There are times when our families give us tremendous joy and happiness, yet others when they can cause us distress and concern. This chapter explores these feelings and looks at how we can manage our families and emotions in a more measured way so we don't become overwhelmed.

My family

I expect it is a long time since anyone asked you to draw your family and I am probably right in thinking it would be much more complicated now than when you were small. We are going to start this chapter with a bit of drawing. You do not need to be an artist to do this, and remember no one is looking! You are going to do three pictures or diagrams.

Exercise: Where am I in my family?

1. Draw a picture of your family, including everyone you see as part of it, pets and all. (Draw them as stick people if you want.) Add any distinguishing features you think are relevant – for example, a walking stick for a parent or a pram for a baby.

2. Now put that aside and draw a circle in the middle of the page and put yourself in the middle. Around your circle place all the people who are in your family. (You may find that more people pop into your mind than you had in the original picture; if that is the case, add them in and just make a note as you may want to come back to them later.) Put those you are close to nearest your circle and those less involved with you further away. Take a look at the picture and note where your relationships lie. Is this how you want them to be? Or, are there people you want to have more contact with than you currently do?

3. Now draw an arrow to and from them. If you are the one who provides care or attention or physical or emotional support, then make the arrow to them bold and the arrow from them dotted. If you are the one who is looked after, then make the arrow to them dotted and the one from them to you bold. If the relationship is equal, the thickness of the lines should be the same. Someone such as a baby may not physically look after you but you are emotionally fed, so in this case the arrow would probably be even. Do this for all the people. Now, in a different colour, add in your friends, again linking them to you by arrows. You now will have a sense of who you receive support from, who you provide support to, and who is important in your world. You can also add in work colleagues if you want the full picture.

4. We are going to end with a family tree. Again, start with your-self and add in all your family including those who you might not see and who are not included in the above diagrams. Go back as far as grandparents and great-grandparents, if you know about them. Finally, circle the blood relatives. For example, your parents would be circled and your in-laws not, your half-siblings circled and step-siblings not.

Take out your notebook.

 Ask yourself
- How did you feel while doing this? What issues did it raise for you?
- Were you aware of people who weren't there because they are no longer part of your life, through death, divorce or disputes?
- Do you get as much support as you give?
- Were there people you forgot in the first diagram and remembered in the second? Why was this? Is there anyone you find a burden?
- What feelings did you notice when you drew your family tree and I asked you to separate the blood relations from the others? Was there a difference in the support you felt you got from them?
- Have things sprung to mind just by doing this that you think need resolving or changing? Make a list of them and jot down a plan of action. For example, 'I haven't spoken to my brother for months so I am going to call this week.'

My hunch is that every one of you will have had feelings stirred by doing this exercise. You may be thinking, 'No wonder I am tired – I do all the giving', or 'There are so many different people in this family, it is hard to keep in touch', or 'My family has become very small and my friends are the people I feel closest to'. Whatever it is, just note it and, as we go through this and the next chapter, you should find ways to improve your family life, if it needs improving.

Making our lives work for us

One thing I do want to point out is that we will be looking at how to make things work better for you, so that you have the best life you can. That does not mean everything will be perfect. You are old enough to know that life has its ups and downs; sometimes it is wonderful and sometimes it is tough. I do not want you to enter a fantasy world and believe it will all be perfect, as you will only be disappointed. That said, you do want your life to be as good as it can be.

But first, let me introduce our last course participant, Stephen. He is 56 and was married for the second time three years ago and has two-year-old twins. He has three older children from his first marriage aged 31, 27, and 24. He also has a two-year-old granddaughter. After doing the drawing exercises he said:

Stephen, 56

'I've been really struggling with my life. At times, I feel as though I cannot get it right, however hard I try. There are so many demands on me. The twins are adorable and I love them dearly but, if I'm honest, I feel overwhelmed. It's no wonder, really. I'll be 72 when they finish school and 75 when they finish university. I know lots of people think I'm irresponsible becoming a father again but I did think it through and so did my new wife. We know I'm old to be a dad. My elder children were somewhat appalled, especially my son. My twins are aunts to his daughter. He feels I've trodden on his territory. I think one baby would have been bad but two is just rubbing it in his face, as everyone makes a fuss of them. I've got a friend who re-married at the same time and he's forever telling me I'm a braver man than him and he's satisfied with the children he has.

'I'm an only child and, in the last two years, my mother has been diagnosed with vascular dementia and my father with prostate cancer. They're both 83, so it's perhaps not surprising but it felt like a shock. They were both fine when the twins were conceived and I was probably burying my head in the sand, just assuming they'd carry on being well. I'm trying to visit them three times a week to check they're all right. I'm also talking to my mother several times a day on the phone as she has become very anxious, she'd like me there every day. Without wanting to sound dramatic, I feel torn in two. I don't know who to attend to first. I never really understood the term 'sandwich generation' before. I knew what the words meant but I thought people were making a bit of a fuss. Not any more. To sum up, I feel exhausted, guilty and stupid because I do not have the answers. I'm going round in circles.'

Pat and Alison (see Chapter 2) are both struggling with their growing and adult children and Alison also has an ill father. They sat and nodded vigorously as Stephen talked. Pat then responded:

Pat, 64

'It's interesting listening to you because we've both done things differently from how I would have expected when I was young. I've no regrets. I'm very happily married now; it's just that we have so many responsibilities and I thought they'd be over by this stage. We're not part of a sandwich, as we have no parents. I feel like we're the toast and the family is the cheese on top! We're still supporting them. If I could say they were lazy or extravagant, it would be different but they're not and yet we're still struggling. I fear the future.'

Alison, 54

Alison added, 'All our situations are different and we're all feeling guilty. My dad can't help ageing but I feel cross with him most of the time and I then feel bad. My kids do their best but it still leaves me like Stephen, stuck in the middle.'

Easy to moan

At that point, I stopped them. The reason I did so was because it felt as though we could be heading for a good old moan! Moaning is fine in small bouts and sometimes useful if you have a good friend who empathizes, listens, and commiserates with your woes. However, it won't get you very far. The truth is that the more you moan without finding solutions to the issues, the more fed up you will become.

I am sure some of what the participants were saying resonates with you and your family situations and you will fully understand how they feel. Some things cannot change, however much we may want them to – for example, it is a fact that Stephen's twin girls are the same age as his granddaughter. And he cannot do anything about that.

Changing our responses

But Stephen can change his response to the situation and in doing so improve things for himself and his family. By using different problem-solving techniques, we can find different solutions (see Chapter 10 on problem-solving). For example, he could look at different ways to manage his parents' care so he is not run ragged.

Guilt

Every single one of the participants at some point in the course talked about feeling guilty. Let us take a look at guilt, which is a universal emotion although some of us are much more prone to it than others. Guilt is the feeling we have when we have done something we think we shouldn't have done or we have not done something we think we should have done. It can leave us feeling sick to the core and anxious, too, as well as unable to move forward and make rational decisions.

There are two sorts of guilt described by psychologists: 'healthy' and 'unhealthy' guilt. Healthy guilt is an appropriate feeling (although the strength of it can sometimes be out of proportion to the event) because it alerts you to the fact you may have done or said something that was not very special and you need to apologize and behave differently in future. An example would be Alison shouting at her children that they do not bring in enough money and they are costing too much to keep. Her guilt alerts her to the fact that she's being unfair and gives her an opportunity to do something about it, such as apologize and then work out together how they can manage the household budget better or help her children to look for better-paid work. Healthy guilt is only useful, of course, if you identify why there is a problem and then rectify it. If we feel bad but do not change our behaviour, we just add to the 'pile of guilt' and wear ourselves down.

Unhealthy guilt usually comes from outsiders or our own critical voice which tells us something is wrong and that we are not living up to the required standard; in other words, the part inside ourselves that ticks us off. An example of this is Stephen feeling guilty he had children who are the same age as his granddaughter. He knows he made a considered decision that was right for him but, equally, knows that others such as his son disapprove. Another is hearing his friend saying, 'I am happy with the children I have and would never consider having any others at my age.' Instead of listening with detached interest to how other people manage their lives, Stephen immediately compares himself to them, decides he has done things wrong, and feels terrible as a result.

Feeling guilty

Is this something you find yourself doing? Is it other people who make you feel bad or is it your inner voice? Many of us find our inner voice is that of our parents we have internalized. This type of guilt does us no good; it lowers our self-esteem and general sense of wellbeing. Often, when others say something that makes us feel guilty, it is because they want us to do it their way and act like them. If you are aware of this, you won't internalize the feeling but just accept they have a different point of view and carry on doing things the way that suits you best. When we do it to ourselves, we need to switch off that inner voice just as you did in Chapter 6.

Let us see what we can do with your guilt. Take out your notebook.

Exercise: Healthy and unhealthy guilt

1. Write down all the things that are making you feel guilty right now.

2. Score them from 1 to 10, with 1 being a little guilty and 10 wracked with guilt.

3. Order them on your page from least guilty to most guilty.

4. Start with your least guilty feeling to get you into practice.

5. Now answer these two questions: (a) Does this feeling make you want to behave differently? (b) If you do behave differently, will it make you feel better?

   If you can answer 'yes' to those questions, it is healthy guilt and gives you an opportunity to change.

   Go back to your list of healthy guilt items.

6. Decide what you are going to do to behave differently and whether there are any other actions you have to take, like Alison who has to apologize to someone.

7. If you need to involve anyone else, then agree a date by when you will do it. If not, just start behaving differently.
   If it is unhealthy guilt, you need to stop indulging those thoughts. That is something else that is easier said than done! So let me tell you about an excellent way to do this.

Exercise: Letting guilt go

1. Write down the list of all the unhealthy guilt items, leaving a large gap between the items (the list might be quite long!).

2. Now cut each into a strip so you have a pile of guilt.

3. This next step needs to be done safely as it involves burning the paper. Find somewhere to do this – outdoors would be good.

4. Take the first one, read it to yourself, light a match and burn it. As it burns, watch your guilt disappear into the sky and be blown away by the wind. Keep the ash.

5. Repeat with all the items so you have a pile of ash.

6. Now put the ash in a bag and, if you have a garden and a favourite plant, go and dig the ash in the ground around the plant. You can do it with a houseplant, too, or you might want to buy yourself a new plant. Your guilt has now been put to good use to nourish the growth of the plant. Each day that you see the plant, feel grateful that it has grown and that everything changes.

Some of you reading this will think it's all too 'new age' and odd. But, before you dismiss it as an idea, give it a go; if you still think it is barmy, do not do it again.

Reassessing my relationships

Let us go back to the diagram you did at the start of the chapter with you in the circle. Having cleared the unhealthy guilt, I want you to look at the arrows. You will probably need your notebook for this.

 Ask yourself
- Are there any that you can change? I expect there were a number of things you were doing out of guilt. This diagram now needs to be guilt-free.
- Write down a list of these activities and decide how you are going to change things. It may involve having a difficult conversation with someone else – for example, Stephen telling his mother he cannot come in each day and talking to her about having a carer (see Chapter 10).
- Now take a look at the lines. Are you getting as much or nearly as much support as you give? If you are only getting a little support for yourself, this is not healthy. For some of you, it will be a habit to give to others and put their needs before your own and do nothing or very little for yourselves.
- Take a look at each of these relationships separately. Sometimes, there is nothing you can do to even up the arrows – for example, if someone is ill, you will be doing the giving. For others, there are things you can do to even things up – for example, instead of always being the one who listens, why not ask your friend for some help with something that's troubling you?

Who do I give to?

At some point, every one of you will be spending time giving to others. For some, this will feel just right, so continue as you are. Others may well find they are lacking emotional support and care and feel under-valued. So many of us find that our time is squeezed between our career, family, friends, and chores. One of my clients recently said to me that she was so exhausted by everything she had to do that, when her closest childhood friend who she had not seen for ten years cancelled a weekend visit, she felt relieved rather than sorry. She realized she was on a hamster wheel and needed to get off. Her life was a series of tasks; even seeing her friend had become a chore and there were few moments of joy.

We get so caught up in doing that we forget how to be and how to have fun. Having little or no time for ourselves often leads to us feeling tired, overwhelmed, burdened, frustrated, and generally out of sorts. We cannot always change how things are in our lives and our relationships but we can change how we are with ourselves. We do not always need others to make us feel good and supported; we can do a lot of this by ourselves for ourselves.

Time for me

Let us take a look at how you can find time for yourself to recharge your batteries. When you are feeling nourished, you will manage your life more effectively, more creatively, and have more energy and fun. A notebook moment!

Ask yourself
- What's stopping you taking time for yourself?
- What would it take to make time for you a priority?
- What activities give you pleasure and joy?
- How can you bring these simple things into your daily life?

Making time for yourself does not mean taking a week out or even a day or half-day. It means giving a little time to yourself each day to do something you enjoy. Start with just fifteen minutes a day. For example, sit having a cup of tea listening to some music you like, do some exercise, go for a walk, cuddle your grandchild, write in your diary, chat on the phone to an old friend, do a little gardening – the list is endless. Try it for a week and see if it changes you, and if so in what way. My hunch is you will feel a lot better. If that's the case, then add another five minutes each week until you have an hour a day to yourself. Check each week how that makes you feel. Once you have mastered this, you can add in an afternoon or evening once a week or fortnight and slowly build up the time so you have what's just right for you. The amount of time needed will be different for different people.

My bucket list

Have you made a 'bucket list' – the things you want to do before you die? The term was coined after a film in which two men who were diagnosed with cancer made a list of the things they wanted to do and gradually completed them all.

If you have not got one, pick up that notebook and make a list. They do not need to be momentous ambitions like climbing Everest. Take a look at your 'bucket list' and decide when you can do at least one of them and then tick it off and set a time for the next. Some will need long-term planning such as a trip to India, whereas others will require little time to arrange such as volunteering to help children read.

My top tips

Taking time for yourself is like many of the things we have discussed: easier said than done. Here are a few tips to help you:

1. Complete a time audit. Do you know where the time goes in a day? Keep track for a week of what you do.
2. At the end of the week, take a look at it and see what could be dropped and what could be done differently.
3. Make a list of priorities and see if the bottom two really need to happen or whether they are just things you are in the habit of doing.
4. Plan short breaks for yourself in the midst of your activities. Even a whole weekend of socializing can feel like a chore if you do not allow enough time to enjoy it.
5. Reduce the time you surf the Internet – it can be addictive!
6. Say 'no' to others when they make a request. Do not always be the person who volunteers to stay late at work to finish something off.
7. Schedule in your diary time for yourself so it is as important a commitment as anything else – in fact, it should be your Number One priority!

Chapter Ten
Modern Relationships

Things are very different on the relationship front compared with in our parents' day. Divorce has become acceptable during our adult lives. It was rare when we were children; most single-parent families came about as the result of the death of a spouse, not divorce. Over-50s marriages are generally more stable than those of younger couples but they are not immune to problems. A growing number of couples aged over 50 are choosing to divorce. Figures from the Office for National Statistics in 2010 revealed that the divorce rate for couples over 50 has risen by 39 per cent since 1981.[1] This is despite a 16 per cent drop in the overall divorce rate during the same period. Many more women are filing for divorce than previously, often when their children have left home and they find themselves spending more time with their partner. They come to realize that they want something different from life. Many men are unaware that things are not going well and suddenly they find themselves single and lonely.

New types of families have appeared, such as blended families, bringing with them step-parents and step-siblings, half-siblings and step-grandparents. These complicated families are difficult to manage, as new boundaries have to be traversed. To cope with the various relationships we now find ourselves in, we often find we need new skills. This can involve us in having difficult conversations and needing to find solutions to thorny problems. In this chapter, we look at relationships and how to manage the trickier moments.

Divorce

In 2010, Saga asked more than 1900 people who had divorced when they were over 50 what the reasons were for their break-up:[2]

- One in four people (25 per cent) said a lack of sex was the trigger for their divorce, while 28 per cent said that their partner was emotionally cold or distant and 27 per cent said they lacked commitment.
- Other factors mentioned included nagging (14 per cent) and meeting someone new (13 per cent), while one in ten (10 per cent) said they simply ran out of things to talk about.
- Men had significantly more issues with step-children, with 12 per cent saying they were one reason for a break-up compared with only 4 per cent of women.

Money and relationships

Saga's poll also explored what the main disputes were when going through a divorce after the age of 50 and found that over half of the battles were caused by financial disagreements rather than emotional problems or family matters. The poll found that maintaining the home (33 per cent) and responsibility for debts (23 per cent) were the main reasons for conflict. More than a third of over-50 divorcees (35 per cent) also said they argued about who was responsible for the break-up.

Step-parenting

Many people embark on new relationships and are in second or third marriages, so step-parenting is common. Some have second or third families, which results in children spanning a large age range. Gone are the days when two parents and 2.4 children were the norm. Nowadays, it is not unusual for a 60-year-old to still have children of school age as well as having step-children and parents/step-parents/parents-in-law to manage. All of this has financial as well as emotional implications.

Gay and lesbian relationships

Another very significant development has been the change in legal status and attitude towards gay and lesbian relationships. Until 1967, it was illegal for two men to have a sexual relationship.[3] There has never been a similar law regarding two women having a sexual relationship. It was not until 1994 that the age of consent for homosexual men was lowered from 21 to 18, and 2000 when the age of consent was equalized at 16 for all sexual relationships in the UK.

The Civil Partnership Act became law in the UK in December 2005. Once registered, civil partners have the same rights as a married couple in relation to wills, inheritance law, capital gains tax, pensions, housing, and immigration. It also provides next-of-kin rights for the couple while each partner has a duty of maintenance for their partner and any children. Each partner has the responsibility to be assessed for child support in the same way as in heterosexual marriages. There are approximately 59,000 civil partnerships in the UK.

According to the Office for National Statistics,[4] there were 2.9 million co-habiting couples in England and Wales in 2012. In 2011, there were 12 million married couples with families, 38 per cent of them with dependent children, the same percentage as for co-habiting couple families.

Living alone

There has also been a large increase in the number of people living alone. Figures show that 70 per cent of older men live as part of a couple as opposed to only 40 per cent of older women. Half of all women over 65 now live by themselves, which can mean for some that they have little or no emotional or practical support in their personal lives. The illness of a partner is also an issue, as is bereavement. Even for those who have good long-term relationships, there will be challenges as they age, as work becomes a less important part of their lives and as their children leave home (see Chapter 12). The other growing group are those who have always been single, a lifestyle choice made by more and more people. They, too, have different challenges to manage as they age.

New style families

As you can see, many of us are living such different lives from the ones we thought we would. We are in the vanguard of our parents' generation and we have no blueprint to follow. It is no wonder that at times we find ourselves struggling a bit.

Take a moment with your notebook to consider the following questions:

Ask yourself
- What is your family situation?
- How is it similar to and how does it differ from what you expected?
- Are there any areas that cause you concern, and if so, what are they?
- What would you like to resolve?
- How would you know things are better?

The last question is a really important one to answer. Often, we know that something is wrong but not how we would like it to be. It is essential when we want to change something that we know the end-result we are looking for (see Chapter 13 for more on this).

Our participants' thoughts

Not surprisingly, an interesting conversation took place between our participants (see Chapters 2, 8, and 9) about the way people lived their lives and their family situations.

Philip, 60

Philip, if you remember from Chapter 2, was living with his step-son and his civil partner, James, who had fathered their son with a lesbian friend. He was aware that, even though he had been around from his birth and fully involved as a parent, he thought of James as the boy's father and not himself. But if you asked his son, he would say he had two dads and one mum. Until he did his family tree (see Chapter 9), Philip had not considered that the reason he did not see the boy as his son was that he was not his blood relation. 'I wonder if that's the reason I find myself resenting that I'm working and James is bringing in less money or if it's just because I'm tired and have had enough. But I'm very fortunate to have a child; it's something I thought I'd miss out on when I realized I was gay as a teenager.'

Pat, 64

Pat then joined in: 'If I'm really honest, I feel differently about my children from my step-children. It's not that I don't love them but just not in the same way. I know my husband feels like me. We just don't talk about it. Instead, we often get snappy with each other, often over an apparently unrelated topic when one or other of us feels the other has been unfair to the kids. I wish we could just talk about it, however difficult it might be – I'm sure we'd manage things better then.'

Stephen, 56

Stephen agreed. 'I've got a problem with my kids, my ex-wife and the relationship my new wife has with my older children and I just don't know how to solve it' (see Chapter 9 for his story).

Susan, 62

Susan chipped in. 'It's interesting because I never wanted to marry or have children. It's only recently that I've started to wonder about it. I have lots of godchildren but I think people become more insular as they get older and fall back on family. I worry about being lonely, so need to do something about managing my later years (see Chapter 12). My main concern at the moment is my relationship with my mother. We're in such a bad way with each other. I'm so angry with her about becoming ill, which is of course ridiculous. Every time we get into a discussion, we end up shouting. I know there's a different way to handle this but just can't work it out.'

Pat, 64

Pat had additional concerns. 'I really worry about money but we're very lucky as we have a big house which is worth a lot. My children will never be in this position. My husband and I bought our house together and he put in a lot more money than me. That was more than 20 years ago. I've worked on the house and managed it and bought things for it over the years. We've both avoided writing wills, which I know is foolish at our age. We just can't decide who should be left what. He feels his children should have a higher percentage of the house's value than my children, and I don't. Of course, this could all be irrelevant, as we may well need to use the money to live on. It's a real problem that we just can't seem to find a way to resolve.'

Sarah, 59

Sarah widened the discussion. 'I worry about the legacy we've left our children. I know there has been lots written about the baby boomer generation being selfish. Listening to us, you wouldn't think so but we've had it good compared to the generations that came before and the generations to follow. I worry that my daughter won't be able to afford anything and will still have to be working well into her old age. It is so much more complicated than it was.'

What about you?

How much of the above resonates with you? Having heard the participants' views, you might want to add to the list of things you would like to change. We may be older but we are certainly still young enough to keep our minds open. You can find more information in the Resources section and the Bibliography at the end of the book.

Relationships running smoothly

Our focus now will be on how we can have the relationships we want and what we can do to help our lives run more smoothly. There are two areas we should look at, one involving difficult conversations and the other problem-solving.

How to have a difficult conversation

Let us start with difficult conversations. Have you ever been in a situation where you know that raising a particular topic at that moment could only lead to upset, and yet you do so? Because of their nature, difficult conversations need to be planned.

Even before you start the conversation, you need to do a number of things:

- Identify what has made you upset/angry/hurt.
- Pinpoint what you want to resolve.
- Work out what needs to happen to make you feel better.
- Plan when it is best to talk. Never attempt a conversation when either of you is tired, short of time, upset by something external or when the event that has upset you has just occurred.
- Tell the other person that you want to talk, ask when would be a good time for them, then agree a time and stick to it.
- Start by asking them how they feel about the situation and let them speak.
- Listen to what the other person has to say – that does not mean you have to agree – and then tell them how you feel.
- If it is a difference of opinion, agree that you both want to come to some resolution before you find yourselves going in the opposite direction.
- Always state your feelings clearly and honestly.
- Try and keep your voice firm, relaxed, and calm.
- If either of you gets over-emotional, then stop the conversation, agree when to resume talking, and take a break.
- Keep talking about it until you come to a resolution.
- If you still cannot resolve things, then seek out a professional to talk to.

It is really important in any relationship at home or at work that you find an open and honest way to talk to other people.

We all know that at times things can be difficult but, in my opinion, most things can be happily resolved as the result of a good conversation. Take out your notebook.

 Ask yourself

Take a minute or two to jot down any conversations you need to have and plan both the outcome and when you are going to have the chat. It is really important to fix a date, otherwise time will fly by.

The art of problem-solving

If we are good at finding solutions to our problems, they will just disappear. Over the years, we all learn techniques for solving problems. Our methods become habits and we find ourselves solving every one in the same tried and tested way. When we are confronted with a problem, we often think about past problems, recall the solution we used, and then repeat it. This is what is known as uncreative thinking, as you are just going for one style and hoping that one size fits all!

Become a creative thinker

To solve a thorny problem, though, you need to become a creative thinker and look at the problem from all aspects. This will enable you to come up with a number of different solutions, which you can test in advance. Sticking with one idea until a solution is found is known as *vertical thinking*.

When *thinking laterally*, you continue to generate ideas even after a promising idea has been produced. A lateral thinker can wander in different directions to find creative solutions and will often be wrong along the way in order to be right in the end. Lateral thinkers welcome and explore seemingly irrelevant facts or ideas, whereas vertical thinkers shut out all irrelevant information.

There are merits to both types of thinking. If you used only lateral thinking, you would be constantly experimenting and broadening your thinking and you would seldom find a solution. If you only used vertical thinking, you could go a long way down the wrong path because you failed to find the correct path before starting out. A good compromise would be to use lateral thinking until you have decided on a solution to the problem and then switch to vertical thinking to implement that solution. Vertical thinking uses logic the traditional way.

Let us try doing some lateral thinking. Take your notebook and attempt the exercise below.

Exercise: Lateral thinking

1. Find a piece of paper and a pen.

2. In two minutes, write down as many different things as you can think of that you can do with a suitcase.

3. Do not limit yourself – anything goes!

4. Now do the same thing for an old tyre.

5. How many ideas did you get?

6. Now apply exactly the same technique to your own problem. I asked Pat to write 'inheritance' on a sheet of paper and then to jot down as many ideas as she could. You do the same. Do not stop yourself because your critical voice says it is crazy, just put down whatever comes into your head.

Problem-solving broken down

There are a number of elements to the problem-solving process:

(a) Problem definition – in other words, understanding the problem.
(b) Idea generation – thinking of as many possible solutions as you can.
(c) Analysis and evaluation of ideas to solve the problem.
(d) Decision-making.

Exercise: What type of problem solver am I?

We have just done (a) and (b) and will come back to the other two parts in a minute. First, have a go at the questionnaire below. It will help to identify some of your problem-solving blocks and the skills you need.

Look at each statement in the table below and decide how strongly you agree or disagree with it. Then circle the appropriate response, where SA = 'strongly agree', A = 'agree', N = 'neither agree or disagree', D = 'disagree', and SD = 'strongly disagree'. Answer all the questions.

Question	SA	A	N	D	SD
1. I can usually understand a problem from other people's viewpoints					
2. I try not to come up with stupid suggestions or ideas					
3. Time spent daydreaming can often help in solving a problem					
4. Most people want pretty much the same out of life					

(continued)

Question	SA	A	N	D	SD
5. Sometimes I have to 'sleep' on a problem before I can make any headway with it					
6. I tolerate 'wild ducks' as long as they all fly in formation					
7. It is worth spending quite a bit of time defining a problem before starting to solve it					
8. I can always spot a winning idea right away					
9. I believe that rules are often made to be broken					
10. I can usually sum up people and situations pretty quickly					
11. I do not mind taking a gamble in trying to work out a way to resolve a situation					
12. Problem-solving is a serious business					
13. I often find it useful to visualize the situation in my mind when trying to solve a problem					
14. Some problem-solving techniques just seem to leave you with dozens of half-baked ideas					
15. I take it as constructive when people criticize my ideas and solutions					
16. I think most people approach problem-solving in much the same way as I do					

Question	SA	A	N	D	SD
17. I often find that the best ideas arise when working under the pressure of imposed deadlines					
18. Every problem can be solved by a combination of cash and commonsense					

Score odd-numbered and even-numbered questions separately: for example, for numbers 1, 3, and 5, a 'Strongly agree' response scores 5, while for numbers 2, 4, and 6, the same response scores 1.

Odd-numbered questions					Even-numbered questions				
SA	A	N	D	SD	SA	A	N	D	SD
5	4	3	2	1	1	2	3	4	5

The questionnaire addresses three types of blocks to your creative thinking:

- Cultural/environmental blocks, type A.
- Perceptual blocks, type B.
- Emotional blocks, type C.

Adding the scores

Add the scores for the appropriate questions to give your total for each of the three types of block, and then add the three to give a grand total:

A	Questions	3	9	15	6	12	18	A score =
B	Questions	1	7	13	4	10	16	B score =
C	Questions	5	11	17	2	8	14	C score =
								Total score =

Let us now look at what these blocks mean and how they affect our approach to solving problems in our lives.

Cultural/environmental blocks

If your score is low in this area, you may have been suscep-tible to cultural and educational influences in the way you tackle problem-solving or maybe there is something in your present environment that is not encouraging you to use crea-tive thinking. Stephen, who is very stressed at the moment, is unlikely to be very creative.

Sometimes our school and family have reinforced a belief that humour, fantasy, and play have little place in either learning or problem-solving. In addition, in our education system a high value is placed on left-brain thinking – reason, logic, analysis – while right-brain thinking – feeling, intuition and qualitative judgement – has, until recently, been the poor relation (see Chapter 12). These factors can have a strong influence on our creative thinking capability.

The influence of our environment may affect us in many ways. It may make us resistant to change, unable to see or do things differently. We can reduce the impact of cultural/environmental blocks by trying some of the following:

1. Use fantasy and daydreaming as part of your problem-solving. Engage your imagination so you can visualize what different solutions would look like and then envis-age how they could be improved.

2. Practise creative thinking techniques and solutions (see the Resources section).

3. Have you got rules or routines that stop you having a fresh viewpoint when you need one? Ask why these rules were set up. Are they still valid and what is their purpose?

4. Bring humour into your problem-solving – as soon as we smile, we feel better.

5. Try not to be defensive if others criticize your ideas or solutions. Respond positively in a way that stimulates further creative thinking.

6. Creative thinking sometimes means throwing away commonsense (within reason!) and being open to irrational or previously unacceptable viewpoints. Sometimes, it is good to be outrageous.

Perceptual blocks

If your score is low in the way you perceive a problem, this indicates that your perception is not so developed as to enable you to make full use of your creative ability. It may be that you tend to define problems too rigidly or specifically. You may be an excellent vertical thinker and not use lateral thinking to find solutions. You probably tend to categorize or label things and are unable to exploit your creativity to the full.

Often this is because our education has emphasized analytical problem-solving methods and fostered the belief that for any problem there is one right answer. My hunch is that is what Pat's husband is doing when they discuss inheritance.

We can reduce the perceptual blocks to our creative thinking by trying the following:

1. Explore a problem from all angles so you really understand it. Be aware that there may be a variety of goals and objectives.

2. Spend some time defining a problem before attempting to solve it. This is very important and the only way you will know what you are going for. Once you've stated the

problem clearly, try to re-state it in at least three different ways. This process alone can give rise to totally unexpected avenues of thought.

3. Do not assume that there is a right way to solve a problem. There are many different approaches, theories, and
   techniques that can help in the creative thinking process.
   Some may work better for a particular problem. Make sure
   that you are open to different approaches.

4. Develop the use of visualization in your problem-solving:
   imagine the problem from every viewpoint and try to see
   what would be happening if a solution were found.

Emotional blocks

If your score is low in this area, there may be some emotional
reasons responsible for the block. Your education or upbringing may have reinforced the belief that not only is there one
answer but that there is only one right answer; hence a fear
of being thought stupid or foolish for not producing brilliant
or perfect solutions immediately. If we let that critical voice
in, we are likely to kill off any fragile and newly formed solutions prematurely.

Creative thinking will sometimes be an unstructured
process. There is often no fixed agreement about the way ideas
are formed. You need to relax a little and give yourself some
time. 'Sleeping on the problem' is not evading the issue but
is in fact a very productive, considered course of action. Simi-
larly, it may mean that you should, from time to time, relax
your mind and allow your heart to determine in what direction
your problem-solving should go. It may be hard but work on
having several ideas before you go for the ultimate one.

You can reduce emotional blocks by trying the following:

1. Allow yourself to have seemingly stupid ideas. This is often hard for us because, as we age, our assumption is we should know it all by now! But sometimes those 'crazy' ideas turn out to be spot on.

2. When stuck on a problem, 'sleep on it' or take a break. Your subconscious will continue to work on it and you may find that new ideas have bubbled up from nowhere.

3. Try to look beyond the first obvious idea that appears to be a winner. Spend time examining alternative solutions.

4. Consider new or unusual solutions. Work on the basis that there is a part of every idea that can be used, either by itself or in combination with other ideas.

5. Do not worry about the quantity of ideas that techniques such as brainstorming provide. They stimulate the brain to produce yet more ideas and increase the likelihood that a different solution can be found.

Revisiting a problem

Go back to the problems/issues you identified at the start of the chapter. Choose the most pressing one and now, knowing a bit more about your style of problem-solving, use a different approach and come up with a different solution. It is often good to brainstorm with someone else, as they will have ideas you would never have thought of.

As discussed at the start of this chapter, we are all living very different lives from our parents and from each other. Learning how to manage this is essential if we are going to have a happy life and achieve our goals. Learning how to have difficult conversations and how to problem-solve, moreover, will enable you to do just this.

Part IV
Your Health and
Wellbeing

Chapter Eleven
Keeping Fit and Looking Good

When I was talking to a friend about writing this chapter, she asked me if I was going to 'go beyond tired and achy joints' that many of us have and if I was 'going to either pretend that ageing doesn't affect our bodies and our minds, or give magical tips as to how to appear ten years younger'.

The truth is I am not going to do any of those things and nor are you! The reason I am not going to bang on about aches and pains is because it would be pointless. Moaning, as we have said before, just creates more misery and certainly will not improve your joints! And there is not any magic formula to hold the years at bay, whatever the adverts might claim.

What we are going to do, however, is look at the facts about ageing so you can dispel some of the myths that may be colouring your perceptions and fuelling your fears. You will already know from reading this book that how we feel inside affects our actions and behaviour. There are tips in this chapter to help you do exactly that.

Age quiz

Let us start with a quiz about health and image and see what you believe is true.

Myth or Reality	Answer True/False
1. Everyone gets dementia – it is a normal part of ageing	
2. Our physical strength declines as we age	
3. Most older people have stopped having sex	
4. Drivers over 65 have fewer accidents than drivers under 65	
5. Chronological age is the most important determinant of the ageing process	
6. The majority of older adults say that they are happy most of the time	
7. There are products on the market that will delay ageing	
8. Over 85 per cent of people over 80 can manage all normal daily activities on their own	
9. As your body alters with age so does your personality and you become angrier, less assertive, and do not like change	
10. A positive attitude and lifestyle can slow the effects of ageing	

How did you do? The even-numbered statements are 'False' and the odd ones are 'True'. I expect you were wrong about a few! Let me expand on the answers to the questions.

Everyone gets dementia – it is a normal part of ageing

FALSE: The chance of developing dementia increases with age. However, dementia is not a natural consequence of ageing and it does not affect everyone. A study undertaken by EURdEm[1] for the Alzheimer Research Trust (see Bibliography) concluded that between 2 and 3 per cent of people aged 65–69 have dementia, which increases to between 8 and 10 per cent for those aged 71–79, around 22 per cent for those aged 80–85, and as much as 50 per cent for those aged 85–99.

Our physical strength declines as we age

TRUE: Physical strength does tend to decline with age. Exercise is extremely helpful in counteracting and limiting the amount of loss. The reality is that a 65-year-old who takes regular exercise probably will be in better shape and have greater physical strength than a 35-year-old couch potato.

Most older people have stopped having sex

FALSE: This is a common myth. Sexual activity continues to be important for many well into their eighties and nineties. Things do change, however. For example, for men the time it takes to get an erection may slow dramatically, while women may experience changes in the amount of lubrication they may experience post-menopause. It is important to see a doctor about any sexual issue, as most can be very easily solved. Our biggest sexual organ is our brain. The first step towards becoming intimate is experiencing sexual desire – a process that starts with the brain. All thoughts, feelings, and bodily sensations correlate with specific nerve cells being activated. Sexuality also includes the expression of feelings and self in a variety of ways in an intimate relationship. It is not confined to intercourse.

Drivers over 65 have fewer accidents than drivers under 65

TRUE: Despite deteriorating eyesight and hearing loss, older drivers are disproportionately safe and less likely to cause accidents. According to the AA, a 70-year-old is as safe as a 25-year-old and an 80-year-old safer than someone in their teens.[2] As we get older, we are much more able to adapt our behaviour to any changes that occur in ourselves and take the necessary precautions.

Chronological age is the most important determinant of the ageing process

FALSE: We all age differently and our chronological age is the least important factor. It just tells us how many years we have been alive. The age that matters is our functional age. There are three factors that make up functional age: psychological, social, and physiological/biological age. How we function in our social environment is of utmost importance. Think of people you know. I am sure you can think of people in their eighties or nineties who are independent, interesting, creative, and manage their lives well.

The majority of older adults say that they are happy most of the time

TRUE: The majority of older adults report high levels of life satisfaction. Saga undertook a survey of 10,000 over-50s in January 2012. They reported that the average happiness was scored between 60 and 70 per cent. Those in their early fifties were marginally less happy than those in their late sixties and early seventies, who scored happiness at 66 per cent and 71 per cent, respectively. Satisfaction in life also appears to improve with age. Those over 65 felt the most satisfied, rating themselves at 68 per cent, while those in their fifties gave a score of 64 per cent. Research from the University of Warwick found that for both men and women in the UK, the probability of depression peaks at around the age of 44.[3]

The more socially active an individual, the higher their life satisfaction. If you are in poor health, whatever your age, you are more likely to be fed up. Of course, that's an over-simplification but there's no doubt that exercise and healthy eating can contribute towards a long life and one of good quality.

There are products on the market that will delay ageing

FALSE: This is a bit of a trick question, deliberately posed to make an important distinction. The majority of scientists agree that the basic biological process of ageing – the genetic, progressive, and detrimental damage that occurs inside our cells – cannot be delayed. On the other hand, most anti-ageing clinicians claim that the physical signs of ageing can and have been delayed or even reversed. So is it really possible to look and feel younger? Let us take skin as an example. There are substances that have been identified that activate skin cell regeneration and reduce wrinkles and can delay or reverse the signs of ageing. In a study performed in Tokyo, researchers found that polyphenols and xanthine,[4] naturally occurring plant chemicals, maintain antioxidant levels and balance hormone levels in the body. The scientists came to the conclusion that 'topical application of plant extracts and xanthine derivatives suppressed wrinkle formation, dermal connective alteration, and collagen accumulation'.

According to a report produced by the Directorate General for Enterprise and Industry (European Commission),[5] we spent £8 billion in 2011 in the UK alone on cosmetic products and that does not include the mushrooming cosmetic surgery industry. And, although women spend more money on these beauty aids, the baby boomer man is interested, too.

Over 85 per cent of people over 80 can manage all normal daily activities on their own

TRUE: Most people over 80 can carry out all their daily activities and have no increased need to depend on others any more than they did at other points during their adult years except when it comes to heavy work such as moving furniture. Of course, if you are ill, it will be different but that's true whatever your age. If you have a serious illness at 40 or 80, you will need support.

It is only the very elderly who may need more help. As we have already seen in Chapters 4, 5, and 6, the older person is still highly capable of learning new things, whether changing career or building their own business. Interestingly, an area that has really benefited from this is volunteering. Older people's volunteering was recently evaluated in a report by ResPublica[6] as being worth £10 billion a year in the UK, while a quarter of all families are estimated to rely on grandparents for childcare, contributing nearly £4 billion a year to the economy as it enables both the children's parents to return to work.

As your body alters with age so does your personality and you become angrier, less assertive, and do not like change

FALSE: We are no more angry or irritated than younger people. If anything, as we age we learn how to manage our moods better. So often you hear people talk about someone in their sixties or seventies as having mellowed. But I am not convinced we change that much. If you were someone who was angry or irritated a lot of the time when you were young, you will probably be someone who is angry or irritated a good percentage of the time when you are older. I remember many years ago being with a group of people of mixed age. One of the younger ones said she was hoping her mother would be kinder when she was older. The wise older facilitator replied, 'If you are an unkind young woman, you will be unkind when you are older'. This is also true for how you respond to change and for rigid thinking and attitude. These also tend to be relatively stable personality characteristics throughout our lives that we fall back on when we are stressed.

However, I also believe we can modify our behaviour and attitude if we do some work on ourselves, even if our basic personality remains the same. We can become more flexible and able to adapt when we are older by using new skills and strategies.

A positive attitude and lifestyle can slow the effects of ageing

TRUE: As we know, we cannot alter the basic bodily changes that occur but we can slow the processes down. To age healthily, we need to make sure our behaviour is healthy

in all areas of our life. That includes what we eat, how physically active we are, and whether we avoid obvious health
risks. Smoking, high alcohol consumption, use of drugs, and
excessive exposure to the sun will have a negative effect on
our bodies. Many of us will have done things in our youth
that we now know might not have been the best for us.

Change the balance

The great thing is that it is never too late to try to redress
the balance. According to a study by the World Health
Organization,[7] the risk of premature death decreases by half
if someone gives up smoking between ages 60 and 75. People
can live longer if they exercise one or more healthy lifestyle
options – not smoking, eating a healthy diet, getting regular
physical activity, and limiting alcohol – according to a study
by the Centers for Disease Control and Prevention published
in 2011. During the study period of 25 years, those who prac-
tised all four healthy options were 63 per cent less likely to
die early. Not smoking was seen to be the most important.

Attitudes and beliefs

Let us now turn to positive attitudes and beliefs. We have
seen in earlier chapters that our beliefs are the building
blocks for our behaviour. If you believe you are hopeless, you
will behave in a way that is unlikely to help you succeed and
so it becomes a self-fulfilling prophecy.

Logical levels

I want to introduce you to a theoretical idea of Robert Dilts
(see Bibliography), which I believe is extremely useful when

we are thinking about making changes to our lives. Start with the sentence, 'I CAN'T DO THIS HERE'. Now read it again, putting the emphasis on a specific word. Do this for each word. Can you see how that changes the meaning? Let us take a look at what each word means when broken down like this.

I – is my identity. It is who I am. It is my core self, my values. When you meet someone new in a social setting, an introductory question is often, 'What do you do for a living?' How do you normally answer? If you do not know, then listen next time you are asked. Some of us say: 'I work at ...'. Others reply, 'I'm a ...'. If you say the latter, you are very identified with your job. It helps to define who you are.

CAN – is a belief. Have you heard people or even said yourself, 'It's impossible but I'll try.' Invariably when we say this we fail! Just by articulating it, we are setting ourselves up for failure. If you really believed it was impossible, you wouldn't try it in the first place. How much better to say, 'I think this will be a challenge and I am good at those so I'll give it a try.' Our beliefs affect what we do and our behavior, too. A salesperson who does not believe in their product cannot sell it.

DO – is a skill. We need skills to do any activity – for example, dancing the tango, sailing a boat or doing an Excel spreadsheet. We need specific skills to do certain activities and without these we are unlikely to achieve our goals. When we find we cannot do something, it is often not because we do not want to but because we do not have the necessary skills.

THIS – is your behaviour. You need different behaviour for different activities. For example, you need to be able to use a computer, type and manage numbers to use an Excel spreadsheet, or learn specific steps for the tango.

HERE – relates to the environment, context, time, and place. There are some things we can do in one place and not another because it is not appropriate. For example, taking your shoes off and wearing slippers when going out to dinner in a restaurant is not on, although it is something you can do very happily at home when you have a meal.

When we think of ageing, we often put a negative spin on it believing it will be bad. You hear people say, 'It's going to be all downhill from now', or 'I've had the best years of my life', or 'It's no surprise I have aches and pains, I'm 62!' If you convince yourself that's how it is going to be, then that's how it will be. Instead, drop that tired old mantra and start saying, 'I'm looking forward to the next stage of my life; it will offer so many opportunities', or 'These next years are going to be the best I've had', or 'A few aches and pains won't stop me doing anything'.

Myths and fantasies

So many myths about ageing are stated as facts that it is no wonder we can become despondent. Fortunately, however, things *are* changing. Older people are being seen as positive role models. Older men and women are now actively being sought in all walks of life, including TV and modelling, which were once the exclusive province of the young. Fashion products are now being created for our age group that allow us to be both our age and fashionable at the same time, without our looking like mutton dressed as lamb.

But I think it is important to make a distinction between old and older. Shifting from older to old will depend on the individual. However, there's a big difference between being 60 and being 90; in fact, the same number of years as between being 20 and 50. We expect a 20-year-old to have very different needs, abilities, interests, and requirements from a 35-year-old let alone from a 50-year-old. And yet, even now when the media talks about age, they tend to lump 60- to 90-year-olds in one group.

I am reminded of when I was asked by the Department of Health not so long ago to comment on some services for those aged 50 and upwards. I am glad they are now aware there's a difference! There is no doubt things will be different when we are 90 from how they are at 50, 60, and 70. It is really important you remember this when thinking about yourself. In the end, of course, it is how you feel that matters.

How we look

One area where we can be very critical about ourselves is our looks. Of course, you will look different in the mirror from how you did when you were younger but often that's no bad thing. Try the exercise below to increase your confidence and to feel really good about how you look.

Exercise: Photo-gazing

1. When you think back over the years, what are the pictures of yourself at different ages? Do you see yourself as glamorous, the most desirable person on earth, and so much better than now, or do you have a rather negative picture of yourself in your youth and feel you look so much better today. Either way, we are going down memory lane. To do this, you are going to have to gather together some photographs.

2. Find one or two from every decade, ideally one taken every five years, because even if our bodies do not change much our hairstyles and clothes do.

3. Lay them out on the table chronologically. Start with the earliest one. Take a good look at yourself and note what you like about the way you looked as well as what was not so special.

4. Do this for all the photos. Make sure you look at hair, clothes, skin, body shape, and your face. Leave your critical voice in the other room while you are doing this so you look for the positives as well as things you are not so keen on.

5. Take your notebook and make a chart as below.

6. Make a list of the good points and not not-so-special ones for each decade up to the present day. Focus on even the smallest features such as your teeth or your long eyelashes or your lovely ankles. I am sure you will have realized that even in your youth you had bits you didn't like.

7. Now copy all the good features on to the next page. I expect you will be surprised how many of the same features are as great now as they were then.

Age	Good points	Not so good points
Under 10		
10–20		
20–30		
30–40		
40–50		
50–60		
60–70		

This list can be used whenever you feel low in confidence or are having a bad-hair day. Take it out and read through all your best features and immediately you will feel so much better. Do not be ashamed about keeping the list in your back pocket or handbag so that you can refer to it at will, and remind yourself that, yes, you are pretty amazing!

MY BEST FEATURES

An example would be:

1. Long eyelashes

2. Slim ankles

3. Winning smile

4. Long fingers

Now make your own list:

1.

2.

3.

4.

5.

6.

I hope you now have some tools that will enable you to focus on yourself and your strengths rather than letting your head run away with itself every time you hear something negative about ageing. I know that it is very easy to do but it is extremely unhelpful.

Chapter Twelve
Getting Older: How to Do it Gracefully

What was your response to the title of this chapter? For many of us, it is 'Yes but ...', or 'I'm not there yet'. We may know this rationally but we do not really want to believe it and it immediately raises concerns for us. We'd probably all go along with Leon Trotsky who said, 'Old age is the most unexpected of all the things that happen to a man'.[1]

This chapter looks at new ideas about how our brain works and changes our moods but, because it is our brain, we're in the driving seat and fully in control. If we go into a dark mood caused by a number of things, including loneliness, we'll find ourselves less able to cope with life. There are exercises and tips here to help you change this and become as effective a person as you can be.

Ask yourself
Take a moment to consider:
- What age are you now?
- What age do you think you will be when you consider yourself old?
- What are your concerns?
- What are you doing about your concerns?

Age over the generations

Every generation ages but the numbers have altered down the years. When Shakespeare wrote, only one in three children made it to 21. When Queen Victoria was on the throne, it was one in two. A study in the *Lancet* in 2011 suggested that half of babies born after 2000 will reach 100.[2] Although many of us won't make it to 100 or beyond, we are likely to live well into our eighties or nineties and what frightens many of us is the quality of our lives when and if we do. We worry that we or our partners will become mentally and physically unwell, suffer from dementia, or find ourselves frail, bedridden and alone because our partner has died. Of course, any of this is possible but it is by no means inevitable. What we can do, though, is change our approach and pre-empt possible problems.

Talking about ageing

Ageing was one of the topics discussed on our course. The participants were very concerned about their later life. Michael was worried about being lonely, as he was now divorced, his children were growing up and would have their own lives, and he did not know if he would meet another partner. Bruce was unsure how he would cope if his wife became ill, as he was not 'very good around the house' and he knew he would be lonely. Susan was concerned that she would not be able to look after herself, that she did not have any relatives who could help her and, as all her friends would have aged too, they would not see her and she'd be isolated.

Pat responded to this saying her concern was that she would become old and infirm and that her children would feel obligated to look after her and she did not want that.

Alison was already struggling to cope with her father and she felt really anxious about her children seeing her decline both mentally and physically. Philip worried about having a stroke and being unable to work and James and his son being short of money. Stephen hated the thought of not seeing his twins grow up, and Sarah was fretting about her financial position, caring for a husband who was unwell, and then being bereaved and being lonely.

Do your concerns resonate with theirs? You may also have listed others that were not mentioned above. As we know, it is inevitable that we will age. The trick is to approach it in a positive way, using your problem-solving skills (see Chapter 10) and not waiting until it is too late to do anything about it.

What struck me as the course participants talked was how anxious and fearful they were about their future. A couple of them said they would approach every new stage in their life with trepidation. Others mentioned that it was hard to see anything positive about ageing. In the Resources section, you will find practical information to help with those concerns.

I will now introduce some recent research by neuroscientists on how the brain works and how this affects our emotional responses. There is a lot of interest in the coaching world about the application of this information, as it will help us to understand our reactions and by doing so offers us more options as to how we can change.

How our brain works

Our brain is a highly complex organ. Paul McLean suggests in his 1991 book *Triune Brain in Evolution* that the brain is divided into three parts. The reptilian brain is the inner and most primitive part and is responsible for all our vital functions such as blood circulation, breathing, sleeping, and muscle control. The limbic system, the next in evolutionary terms, emerged in the first mammals and governs our emotions, management of our feelings, our relationship with the external world, and holds our memory of positive and negative experiences. It is where we make value judgements that affect our behaviour, usually unconsciously. The third is the neocortex, which evolved in primates and is largest in humans. Made up of four lobes, it controls our cognitive functions such as thinking, reasoning, imagination, and speech. The three parts of the brain are connected via numerous pathways through which they influence each other.

The other important piece of brain structure to understand is that the brain is divided into two halves down the middle, connected by a bridge of fibres whose role is to enable the two parts to work together. The left brain's focus is on logical, rational, detailed, practical, and structured thinking, whereas the right brain's focus is on creative, abstract, intangible, imaginative, and big-picture thinking (see Chapter 3 and how this relates to managing change).

The brain's gatekeeper

Within the limbic system are two almond-shaped structures called the amygdalae. They act in effect like a gatekeeper whose role is to assess what is entering and whether it is of any danger or concern. They can do this in two ways: by responding immediately without our being conscious of this activity, and by checking for danger and then directing the incoming information to the right part of the cortex. If danger is perceived, the brain is alerted and all resources are activated, including secretion of the hormone cortisol which affects our physiology and puts us on alert. If the incoming information is not of concern, a different reaction occurs – such as pleasure at seeing someone – with different hormones, including serotonin, being released. For example, if you hear an unexpected sound in your house at night, you immediately feel fearful, but as soon as you recognize the steps as those of a family member, you relax and feel fine.

The brain and social interaction

David Rock, a cognitive social neuroscientist, says in his article 'Managing with the brain in mind', that it is now known through many studies that the human brain is a social organ. Its physiological and neurological reactions are shaped by social interactions.[3] When we are exposed to something unexpected, our neurons and hormones are triggered to help ascertain whether this is a potential reward or potential danger. If it is a potential danger, a response occurs that takes blood, oxygen, and energy away from the part of the brain we need most if we are going to process information and be analytic about the situation. Instead, the limbic brain uses our past memories, not the present event, to judge the situation and thus reduces the capability of our brain just when we need it to be working at its best.

I was talking with a client recently whose daughter was travelling on her gap year. They had an agreement that her daughter would contact her on a weekly basis. When her daughter did not get in touch, she started to worry. Two days after the deadline, she said she was unable to do any of her normal tasks; even making a cup of tea was too much, as she was overwhelmed by her fear. But when an email from her daughter arrived, she was able almost immediately to function normally once more.

Connections with others

In *A General Theory of Love*, Lewis *et al.* suggest that our nervous systems are not separate or self-contained and, from birth onwards, our limbic brain is affected by the people closest to us. For example, if you live with someone, you might be able to tell by the way they put their key in the door what kind of mood they're in. When our systems synchronize with one another, it has a profound effect on our personality and life-long emotional health. This is known as limbic regulation. So, if you know the person coming to see you is not in a good mood, you can change your behaviour accordingly.

We learn these patterns early on. Our first attachments are usually with our mothers and, when our limbic system feels loved and cared for, the hormone oxytocin is produced, which makes us feel pleasure. Oxytocin is also produced when, for example, we are sexually stimulated or praised. When we are not in resonance with someone or we feel fear, we produce cortisol, which is known as the stress hormone. As we develop, we learn patterns of response. The brain likes familiarity and creates neural pathways, which we go down automatically when we perceive something as a known event. The brain often goes for the easiest option when we are faced with something similar, which means we can repeat patterns that are not good for us.

The brain's adaptability

It has been shown by neuroscientists that the brain has plasticity and is capable of making new neural connections whatever our age. These can change and this is known as limbic revision. The brain functions best when it is aware of its own processes and is mindful of what's happening, something that can occur only when you are feeling calm and can concentrate.

When the mind is in this state, it is able to create new neural pathways, which allow new thoughts, ideas, and beliefs to evolve and limbic revision to occur. Many of us know from our life experience that, if you are in a good relationship at home or at work, you feel good. If you are in a bad relationship, you feel lacking in energy, ideas, you are demotivated, and you feel miserable.

In 2009, a very interesting study undertaken by Derek M. Isaacowitz and Fredda Blanchard Fields[4] showed that older adults are more able to regulate their emotions than younger people. The over-55s were much more likely to focus on positive outcomes than those under 25. This is a very good example of neuroplasticity: how we can change the way we respond. The Bibliography lists some articles and books for those interested in how the brain works and how it affects our emotions.

The reason I have spent some time explaining this to you is that by understanding the process that occurs when we become fearful about growing old or our partner dying, we can make different choices about our behaviour. If we become stressed and anxious we are creating the opposite conditions needed to those that will help us to manage these unknown and sometimes difficult situations. Uncertainty sets off all the negative responses that will shut down our creative brain. Learning how to manage our brain is essential in helping us deal with new events.

Now you know what happens in your brain when your emotions change. The next step is to learn how to manage these changes yourself. The following exercises will help you do just that. I suggest you follow them in the order they are presented.

Let us start by looking at how to reduce fear and put your brain into a resourceful state; you will need your notebook for this.

Exercise: Old fears

A good way to start is to think about things in your life that once made you frightened or stressed but no longer do.

1. Make a list of at least five things that frightened you or stressed you in the past – for example, driving on a motorway, swimming in the sea or making a meal for six.

2. Take the first one and think back to when you were first frightened or stressed about it. Run through the scenario in your head from when you had the fear until it was gone. Imagine you are back there in the same situation. What helped you lose that fear? Once you know the answer, jot down the components. Also, make a note of anything that hindered you and made it more difficult to shake off this fear.

3. Repeat the above for all your old fears and stresses.

4. You now know what strategies helped you in the past and what will not be useful in the future.

5. How can you access this information now? Did you find help from a book, the Internet or an advisor or through talking to a friend? Use these strategies now so you can begin to plan what to do to calm your emotional responses and put yourself into a resourceful state.

Once you have completed the above exercise, have a go at the next one; it will help you to see the fear differently. You will need your notebook again.

Exercise: Making fear work positively

1. When you think about ageing, what happens to your body? What are the sensations you experience, such as a dry mouth or a churning stomach? Where does the fear sit in you body? It may be in your shoulders, or give you a backache or headache.

2. If you were to give it a colour, what would it be? Does it have a sound, a taste or a smell? If so, identify them. The more physical qualifies you can give it, the easier it will be to dismiss them.

3. Now imagine a circle in front of you (like you did for building confidence in Chapter 5). Within this circle is fearlessness. Walk into the circle and think of a time you tackled something without any fear, when you used your inner resources to guide you through. You activated positive emotions and your limbic brain worked with you to help you to succeed. Take yourself back to that time and be there as if it were now. Feel all those great feelings.

4. Repeat the above step with another two situations.

5. Now focus on one of the issues that concerns you about ageing. As soon as you think about it, your fear and stress reactions kick in automatically. As we now know, we can change this. Climb into your fearlessness circle and put on all those positive feelings you had when you were thinking about good situations. How do you feel now? Repeat this part of the exercise five times until you are able to meet the challenge and your debilitating fear has gone.

6. Test your fear by trying to re-create it. What colour is it now? Does it still have a sound, smell or taste? Even if it is lingering a little, it will have much less power.

7. Whenever you feel stress or fear, just get into your circle and experience that feeling of calm.

I want to be very clear that this exercise will not change a situation – for example, Alison is having a difficult time managing her father's ageing and is concerned about her own. If she focuses on the negatives and imagines them as though they were here now, she will find herself feeling terrible. But if she reduces her fear and then uses all her abilities to look at solutions, she will be able to face down her demons.

Michael, meanwhile, may not be able to conjure up a partner but, if he's serious about wanting to reduce the possibility of loneliness, there are things he can do now. If he's spending a lot of time alone at home, I can pretty well guarantee he'll get exactly what he fears: loneliness.

Loneliness

Many people worry about being lonely when they're older, and over half of our participants raised this concern. By putting things in place now, it is much less likely to happen. Loneliness is not the same as being alone. It is an emotional state where we feel overwhelmingly isolated and empty. When we are lonely, our self-esteem is low and we are often convinced it is somehow our fault. It is more than just a longing for company or someone to do something with. We often feel socially unskilled, inadequate, less assertive, and unable to make any changes.

Types of loneliness

Every one of us will at some point in our lives experience loneliness. Robert Weiss, in his book *Loneliness: The*

Experience of Emotional and Social Isolation, defines two types of loneliness.[5] Some people rarely feel lonely but, when they do, it is defined as state loneliness – in other words, how you feel at that moment. This loneliness is generated more by the environment than the person and by temporary circumstances that rarely last long.

At the other extreme, the person experiences loneliness all the time, as an inescapable part of their existence, which Weiss defined as trait loneliness. This type of loneliness is generated from within the person although particular circumstances might aggravate it. The real problem comes when the feeling goes on too long and we move from loneliness to depression. When depressed, it is hard to activate yourself to do anything about it. Loneliness is not one single, simple thing; there are both different degrees and causes. It is possible to talk about three different kinds of loneliness: circumstantial, developmental, and internal.

Common causes of loneliness

Divorce, bereavement, retirement, and unemployment are common causes of loneliness. If your partner or the job that boosted your self-esteem and made life meaningful suddenly disappears, then everything can feel hopeless and futile. Often things happen at once – for example, retirement, the death of a spouse or close friend, and a move to a new home. You may find yourself feeling overwhelmingly bleak. As you get older, you may have no close family nearby to turn to for companionship and you may become wary of going out alone. This is circumstantial loneliness. Internal loneliness is when the feeling comes from inside you. It often occurs when our self-esteem is low. At these times we get no satisfaction from others and we feel misunderstood. If you ever feel like this, it would be really useful to talk with a professional who will help you to understand why this is happening and to help you to change your mindset.

Development of loneliness is our learned reactions to loneliness. Our reaction to circumstantial or situational events is somewhat dependent on earlier socio-emotional experiences (that is, our limbic system comes into play), so our developmental loneliness will determine our circumstantial loneliness and our reactions.

Planning ahead

If you are someone who gets lonely or who fears it in the future, now is the time to put things in place to reduce the likelihood. Before I give you my suggestions, take out your notebook and write down as many different ways as you can think of to reduce loneliness. If you find it difficult to do this for yourself, imagine a friend has come to you and asked you to help them to feel less lonely. What would you suggest? Below are a few ideas that the participants and I came up with.

Our practical ideas

- Some of us seek out social occasions to make us feel good. It is likely that at some point in our lives we will spend more time on our own. Like any new activity, it is good to learn to be alone and to practise spending some time learning being relaxed in your own company. It may be uncomfortable at first but I think you will be surprised how much you can enjoy your own company.
- Take up a technique that can help you relax, for example yoga or meditation.

- Spend time concentrating on something that really interests you, such as reading, walking or listening to music. Focus on the pleasure it gives you and note that good things can be done alone.
- Join groups or classes that are local. Many of us find we have friends from work and from different periods of our life who may live some distance away. Start to get to know your local community so you can meet people easily and just drop in on each other. Of course, you need to do something that interests you in the first place, so join a book group if you like reading or a wine-tasting group if you like wine.
- If you have spare time on your hands, think about whether you could spend a few hours working as a volunteer. Are there causes that interest you and which you feel are particularly worth fighting for, or a political cause you would like to become involved in?
- Contact people you have not seen for a while – either friends or family – so you keep your social network alive. Many of us find we see the same few people because we are busy or lazy. A larger social network gives you an opportunity to see people.
- Get a pet. This may sound odd but so many of the people I have worked with have said that when they were bereaved, knowing there was 'someone' there made all the difference.

This list is not comprehensive and you may well have better ideas yourself. The important thing is that, rather than waiting for the fear to happen, you do something about it now so it won't materialize. One of my recent clients was concerned about her mother who was now frail and forgetful. For years, they had talked about her moving somewhere more manageable – perhaps into sheltered housing – but they had missed the boat, as her mother was no longer able to cope. It is very easy to put off dealing with the things we fear because we shut down the resourceful part of our brain. Armed with the knowledge you now have about your physiological responses and exercises and tips about how to check your fears and change things, you should be able, more often than not, to nip a problem in the bud.

Chapter Thirteen
Setting Realistic Goals and Aspirations

This is probably the most important chapter in the book and I would like to explain why. Doing exercises and learning new procedures are all well and good but, on their own and if not followed up, they do not have a lasting effect and will therefore not enhance your life as much as they could.

Making lasting changes

Those of you who have been successful at losing weight or becoming fit will know that you have to put several things in place to achieve your goals. I am reminded of one of the 'quick wins' I was seduced into believing would work forever when I wanted to lose weight. Covered in mud and wrapped in cellophane I lay under a plastic sheet and an electric blanket to enhance the geothermal effect of my body temperature. Amazingly I lost the two inches round my waist as advertised. Perfect if I had wanted to get into that too-tight dress or trousers bought for a special occasion but no good for the long term, as it lasted no more than a day. The real achievements happen when we work steadily to reach our desired goals and then maintain them.

Step by step

Another important thing to remember after you have absorbed a lot of new information is that you cannot work on everything at once. I am sure you've either been in this position yourself or known others who have been enthused by new ideas and tried to implement them all at once, which inevitably leads to overload and often to giving up.

I was talking to a business client recently who had asked two of his team to attend a course on interpersonal communication, as they were not the easiest people to work with. They came back with lots of ideas and proceeded to tell everyone how they should behave and to implement them all at once. Their colleagues reported that they seemed unreal and also rather demanding. Within a couple of days, they reverted to their old ways of behaving and my client, their boss, felt he had wasted his money.

Goals

Let us take a moment to look at goals. It seems to me that over the years we have become a much more goal-focused society and that sometimes we can get fixated with achieving a goal without really knowing what it will do for us. When we set a goal that does not meet our needs fully or help us to be who we want to be, we're often faced with disappointment and a sense of failure since, even when we have met it, we discover it was not the real goal after all.

It has already been noted that we are living longer and healthier lives and that those of us in our fifties and sixties may well have 30-plus years of active life in which to achieve so much. So, working out what it is that you want to do and a plan to get yourself there is going to be essential.

Your goals

Write down all the things you want to achieve over the next 30 years – we will whittle it down in a moment. I asked the participants on my course to do this, too. They came up with a long list that included: studying for a degree, going up in a hot air balloon, learning a language, teaching English as a foreign language, getting fitter and thinner, starting their own business, looking after grandchildren, working for a cause they believed in, becoming a GP, training as a teacher, learning to swim, backpacking across India, becoming the chief executive of a charity, changing career, taking up bridge and photography, moving to the seaside, becoming a potter, studying history, becoming proficient on the computer, becoming a local councillor, getting a dog, and understanding the stock market. The list seemed endless.

Objectives - setting

In Chapter 2, I introduced you to a means of helping you create a good goal often used in coaching and in business that originated in an article in *Management Today* by George T. Doran entitled 'There's a S.M.A.R.T. way to write management's goals and objectives'. S.M.A.R.T. stands for Specific, Measurable, Achievable or Agreed, Relevant, Time-bound. A more recent version, which we discussed, is SMARTER, more powerful and relevant for the modern world because it includes the essential philosophical aspect: Specific, Measurable, Agreed, Realistic, Time-bound, Ethical and Exciting, Reviewed.

Stephen's objectives

As objectives-setting is such an important skill to have, I would like to run through an example using the goal suggested by course participant Stephen. He said he wanted to become a GP. Let us apply SMARTER and see if it meets the criteria.

- Specific – Yes, it is clear that is what he wants to do.
- Measurable – He will know in five years (as long as he has A levels) that he has qualified.
- Agreed – It would need to be agreed by him, his family whose lifestyle might change, and the university that has offered him a place.
- Realistic – There are no set age limits for entry to medical school, although they will take account of the length of training in relation to the length of service you could provide. As he is 56 and it takes five years, he'll be 61 before he qualifies and then it is another three years to qualify as a GP (this is likely to change to five) so, at a conservative estimate, he will be 64 when he becomes a fully fledged GP. Moreover, if a ruling in the Supreme Court becomes law, he'd have to retire at 70. Armed with this knowledge, he now needs to make a decision as to whether it is realistic to proceed.
- Time-bound – Yes, he knows how long it takes.
- Ethical – Well, some might feel it would be a waste of money to pay for his education when he is likely to practise for such a short time, whereas others could argue it is right and proper as we need to eradicate age discrimination and we could do with some older doctors.
- Exciting – Most definitely, if that is his ambition.
- Reviewed – Each year there would be assessments so his progress would be monitored.

Time for another notebook moment.

Exercise: Applying SMARTER

Having reached the end of the book, take your final list of goals and apply SMARTER to each one individually. I expect this will reduce your list. For example, Pat said that she would like to be a millionaire and not worry about money. The others all agreed but you cannot apply SMARTER to that. She may be lucky and win the lottery but she cannot plan for it other than buying a ticket!

Goal fit

Having done SMARTER, I then asked Stephen how becoming a doctor fitted into his life and what was important to him. How would he like his life to be? 'When my older children were young,' he said, 'I spent very little time with them. I was a traditional father and went out to work early and came home late. I really regret that. Now I have the twins, I've got an opportunity to spend time with them growing up. And then, of course, there are my elderly parents. So, even if it were possible to qualify as a doctor, it wouldn't give me what I wanted in my life so it is off my list.'

Take your notebook and list of goals to which you've applied SMARTER and answer the following questions:

Ask yourself
- Would doing this activity fit into my life?
- Which of my values and beliefs would it meet?
- Would it fit with other goals or are they opposed to each other?
- What really matters to me?

Prioritization

Now prioritize and make a list with Number One being the most important. In their book *A Theory of Goal Setting and*

Task Performance, Locke and Latham suggest five principles for setting goals:

1. Clarity – which we have already discussed in relation to SMARTER.

2. Challenge – the level of challenge is important. If you aim for something easy, you'll get little sense of achievement. However, do not go to the other end of the spectrum and make it so hard it is unrealistic. As Bruce said on the course, he'd love to climb Everest but, because of certain health problems, that would not be possible.

3. Commitment – how many of you have made a New Year's resolution and broken it by 2 January? If it is going to happen, you need to be determined and stick with it.

4. Feedback – this is much like the review we talked about earlier: monitor your progress and ask others' opinions. If you are going to start your own business like Marcie (see Chapter 6), you'll need advice along the way.

5. Task complexity – we can sometimes make things too complex and become stressed. Give yourself enough time both to achieve your goal and to make sure you have the necessary knowledge.

Planning

Alison, 54

This leads me to planning. Alison said that she felt she never had any me-time. She wanted to develop a hobby she could do by herself where she could tap into her creative side that she did not use at work. She was interested in pottery, perhaps as a part-time job when she retired. Until now, she would have talked about it and not done anything more. Having completed the other exercises, she decided the time was right and that what she needed was a plan. She decided to do the following:

- Write down the goal in SMARTER terms.
- Identify the factors that would help to achieve this goal starting with finding out where and when local classes were held.
- Decide each of the steps that needed to be undertaken to meet the goal.
- Explore the career pathway.
- Assess that her plan fitted with her lifestyle and values.
- Draw up a time frame for each stage.

Goal ladder

As you will appreciate, achieving a goal usually needs to be done in several stages. This has been described as the goal ladder: you go up one rung at a time until you reach your ultimate goal. Even if it is a one-off event like climbing a mountain, you still need to do the planning first.

So go back to your notebook and write down your plan for the goal you've decided to pursue. Once you have achieved this, you can then start on the next. Many us get into the habit of trying to achieve things on our own when, if we stopped for a moment to think, we could get some help from others.

Susan, 62

Susan, for example, was frustrated as she did not feel she could travel and work abroad because of her mother. She thought her sister was too busy and therefore she was trapped. When questioned, it transpired that she hadn't asked her sister; she had just made an assumption. As Oscar Wilde said, 'When you assume, you make an Ass out of U and Me'.[1] Assumptions sabotage effective communication and more often than not lead you down the wrong path. Susan may be right but she did not know what her sister's reaction would be. Also, when we explored this further and started to look at who could support her in achieving her goal, she came up with several names, including two cousins and an aunt who she thought would be happy to help her mother.

None of us has to do things on our own. There are always people who can support us. These include friends and family, professional advisors, not to mention specialist books and the Internet. Get the notebook out once more.

 Ask yourself
Go back to the goal you have chosen to work on and answer the following questions:
   – Who can provide me with support and help?
   – How would I like that support to be given?
   – Who will be my 'external conscience' to which I give explicit 'nagging rights'?
   – How will I celebrate?

Celebrating our success

You may think the third question is a bit odd. Often, we put off doing things we need to do and require a nudge from someone else to get us back on the right track. If someone nags us, we get fed up, like children who are constantly told to go and do their homework. However, if we agree that someone can gently remind us, this becomes supportive and useful. The last question is equally important. How often have you achieved something, shrugged your shoulders and said, 'Well that's done, what next?' without pausing for breath? Now is the time to celebrate your successes and, if you do, you'll find you start to live the life you love at 50+.

Last thoughts

Just before I leave you to work on the areas in this book that interest you and that will enhance your life, I want to return to a couple of the things I said in the Introduction. For many of us, our lives have not turned out as we imagined when we played make-believe families with our friends as children. A lot will be so much better than we imagined while bits will feel less than special. That is true for all of us, even the people who write books like this!

My story

I truly believe it is possible to change our behaviours and beliefs. We may not change our essence but we can change how we manifest in the world. Like you, I have my struggles that I manage very well at times, less well at others when I revert back to old patterns of behaviour. I am reminded of a time many years ago when one of my children was 12 and was furious that I would not let him do something. Instead of being the quiet thoughtful woman I often am, I reverted to being a child myself and, by the end of the argument, I am not sure which of us was behaving more childishly!

By looking back at incidents like that one and thinking about what I could have done differently, I've learnt to change my behaviour and, most of the time, have the life I love. I truly believe you can do that too. I have not done it on my own. I have had enormous support from my friends and family, professional advisors and of course my clients and course participants, who have taught me so much.

Future support

If you are a coach, I hope these exercises and ideas will enable you to work more effectively with your clients and have given you the opportunity to explore ideas about your own ageing. And, if you think I can be of any help, just get in touch. I would be delighted to work with you to ensure your every success. Take a look at my website for both coaching and workshops (www.experiencematters.org.uk).

Resources

General

http://www.50connect.co.uk
Information, articles, and links to other relevant websites on finance, health, travel, food and drink, genealogy, and so on.

http://www.adviceguide.org.uk
The Advice Guide from the Citizens Advice Bureau provides information on rights, benefits, housing, family matters, employment, debt, consumer and legal issues.

http://www.agepositive.gov.uk
A government run site offering information and advice, focusing on age discrimination and rights in employment.

http://www.ageuk.org.uk
Information, advice, and articles for the elderly about benefits, care, age discrimination, redundancy, business success, support and training, retirement, default retirement age, funding, volunteering, changing careers, setting up your own business, and computer courses.

http://www.bacp.co.uk
British Association of Counselling and Psychotherapy is a charity working towards the promotion and regulation of counselling and psychotherapy, providing information, training, and a therapist directory for counselling and psychotherapy.

http://www.bbc.co.uk
News, entertainment, lifestyle, knowledge, and sport website with information and news articles about ageing, health, relationships, and links to many specialist sites, as well as a section relating to the over 50s.

http://www.gov.uk
A government run website offering a place to find government services. It provides information on housing, local services, money, tax, travel, employment, law, health, education, learning, returning to work, legislation, and benefits. There is a specialist section for the newly retired, and advice on developing new skills.

http://www.engagewithyou.com
Mutual Insurance website with an online magazine, promoting a community for those in the hectic 'middle of life', to share experiences, talk with others, and get help and information when needed.

http://www.enjoy50plus.co.uk
Directory of resources for the 50+. A useful site offering solutions to and information on all sorts of issues, including holidays, travel and financial advice.

http://www.experiencematters.org.uk
Experience Matters Ltd is a coaching and consultancy organization dedicated to the 50+, running workshops, seminars and events, coaching (face-to-face, by telephone or online), information and readers' problems answered. Day events such as: Health and Wellbeing, Career and Personal Development, Looking and Feeling Good.

http://www.laterlife.com
Very useful information portal for people in 'later life' providing advice, ideas, and features on starting your own business,

workshops, retirement planning, pre-retirement, keeping healthy and fit, and holidays.

http://www.maturetimes.co.uk
The *Mature Times* is an online newspaper with articles and news on a wide variety of topics affecting and of interest to the over-50s.

http://www.nhsdirect.nhs.uk
National Health website with information on health and emotional issues, including a 24-hour telephone helpline. There is a specialist section for the 50+, covering empty nest, menopause, and ageing health issues.

http://www.relate.org.uk
Relationship counselling organization offering advice, support, and counselling for managing relationships, including a telephone helpline. It offers sex therapy, workshops, mediation, consultations, and support, both face-to-face and by phone.

http://www.saga.co.uk
Saga is an online organization for the 50+. Provides links to information on all insurance products, money, holidays, health and care, latest news, and a magazine.

www.statistics.gov.uk
A government website compiling statistics on age composition, marriage, births, divorce, and employment.

Chapter 1

http://www.familyandparenting.co.uk
An independent charity with the aim of making the UK a better place for families and children. Publications and reports are available; provides general information, articles, help and advice on being a parent.

Chapter 4

http://www.niace.org.uk
The National Institute of Adult Continuing Education. A non-governmental organization promoting adult learning with useful links for older adults of all walks of life and ability.

http://www.u3a.org.uk
The Third Age Trust is the national representative body for the Universities of the Third Age (U3A), which are self-help, self-managed lifelong learning cooperatives for older people no longer in full-time work, providing opportunities for their members to share learning experiences in a wide range of interest groups and to pursue learning not for qualifications, but for fun.

http://www.centreforconfidence.co.uk
The Centre for Confidence and Well Being works for cultural and social change, offering events, support, resources, and information on positive ageing.

Chapter 5

http://www.inmyprime.co.uk
In My Prime is a specialist consultancy offering advice, strategic guidance, and practical input to employers, marketing organizations, policy-makers, and older people. It covers issues relating to the employment and management of older workers, helping them to devise, implement, and evaluate new ways of managing and developing what can often be a much under-utilized and under-valued resource.

http://www.taen.org.uk
The Age Employment Network promotes an effective job market, which works for people in mid and later life.

Chapter 6

http://www.gov.uk
The government's online resource for businesses, with information, support, compliance, and practical advice on setting up a business.

http://www.experience-matters.org.uk
Experience Matters for business. Offers business support, coaching, executive coaching, consultancy and training, and management solutions for organizations.

http://www.prime.org.uk
The Prince's Initiative for Mature Enterprise (PRIME) helps people over 50 set up businesses for themselves. PRIME's main goal is the relief of unemployment, particularly through helping people become self-employed.

http://www.skilledpeople.com
A small, independent company that is self-funded and connects small businesses wanting to expand and improve with skilled, experienced people who add value and quickly become productive.

Chapter 7

http://www.gov.uk
The place to find government services all in one place. A useful portal site for the over-50s, with specialist information on planning for retirement, finance, training courses and funding, financial support, pension information, and tax advice in retirement.

Chapter 8

http://www.applausestore.com
A one-stop-shop for thousands of free television and radio audience tickets. A free service to see music, comedy, chat, sitcom, reality and award shows produced at many different studios and locations all around the world.

http://www.bbc.co.uk/tickets
The BBC involves all sections of their audience in making shows. Apply for tickets to watch many television and radio productions and shows, all for free, including tours of the studio, and to participate as members of studio audiences.

http://www.gvi.co.uk.
Global Vision International is a non-political, non-religious organization, which runs over 100 projects in 25 countries. Involves environmental research, conservation, education, and community development.

http://www.inspiredbreaks.co.uk
Provides travel advice and support for grown-ups thinking of taking a career break or just looking for a more inspired way to use their annual leave. They offer work with communities, conservation programmes, and exciting adventure tours worldwide.

http://www.seefilmfirst.com
See films for free. Register for free and apply for tickets.

www.volunteersabroad.com
Part of the Cactus group, offering placements of various lengths for travel and work experience that combine language learning with volunteering.

Chapter 10

http://www.stepinasap.co.uk
StepIn ASAP (Advancing Stepfamily Awareness in Practice). An organization of psychotherapists and related practitioners that offers support to people to understand the fundamental challenges for people living in families where not all members are biologically related.

Chapter 11

http://www.50plushealth.co.uk
50+ health and wellness, information on good forms of exercise, discussions, links, alternative ideas and products, plus statistics and advice articles.

http://www.alzheimers.org.uk
The Alzheimer's Society is a leading care and research charity for people with all types of dementia, their families and carers. It provides information about different forms of dementia, help for carers, news and events, telephone help and advice lines.

http://www.bhf.org.uk
British Heart Foundation website with support, information, advice on healthy eating, staying active, and the prevention of heart disease.

http://www.gestaltworks.co.uk
Psychotherapy counselling to help find solutions to stepfamily relationships and changing families, couples relationships, parenting, mediation, resolutions to dilemmas and difficulties.

http://www.icaa.cc
International Council on Active Ageing (ICAA) embraces, rather than fights, the ageing process, opting instead to

improve this experience by promoting health, preventing disease, and encouraging living life to the fullest.

http://www.mentalhealth.org.uk
Mental Health Foundation, with a section for older people, is the UK's leading mental health research, policy, and service improvement charity.

Notes

Introduction

1. Ware, B. (2011) *The Top Five Regrets of the Dying: A Life Trans-formed by the Dearly Departing.* London: Hay House, p. 37, Regret 1.

Chapter 1

1. Quotation by Ignacio López de Loyola – knight, hermit, priest, and theologian born in 1491.
2. Whitman, P. (1953) *Speaking as a Woman.* London: Chapman and Hall.
3. Survey data from Spencer, S. (2005) *Gender, Work and Education in Britain in the 1950s.* Basingstoke: Palgrave Macmillan.
4. Klett-Davies, M. and Skaliotis, E. (2009) Mothers, childcare and the work–life balance, in S.A. Hunt (ed.) *Family Trends: British Families since the 1950s.* London: Family and Planning Institute.
5. Statistics retrieved from Benson, H. (2003) *UK Marriage Statistics.* Available at: http://www.2-in-2-1.co.uk/ukstats.html (taken from ONS data for England and Wales).

Chapter 2

1. The first known use of the term appears in Doran, G.T. (1981) There's a S.M.A.R.T. way to write management's goals and objectives, *Management Review*, 70(11): 35. Available at: www.ebsco.com. See Locke's Goal Setting Theory: Understanding SMART Goal Setting at www.mindtools.com/pages/article/newHTE_87.htm.

Chapter 3

1. www.retrowow.co.uk/retro_collectibles/80s/mobile_phone. html. An online information resource covering the 1930s to 1990s. Changes in the workplace. Articles on history of retro furniture, fashion, and collectables.
2. www.birchills.net/blog/bid/47098/The-history-of-office-life-in -the-fifties, by kind permission by David Hill of Cloudnet. History, blogs, articles, photos, biography – growing up and life in the 1950s and 1960s. Changes in technology.
3. See www.margolis.co.uk/news/office-equipment/office-equipment -through-the-decades-the-1960s, Margolis business systems. News item/blog – office equipment through the decades: 1960s.
4. Eales-White, R. (1994) *Creating Growth from Change: How You React, Develop and Grow*. Maidenhead: McGraw-Hill, p. 28.

Chapter 4

1. Gillard, D. (2011) *Education in England: A Brief History*. Available at: www.educationengland.org.uk/history. Articles, features, history documents.
2. See www.legislation.gov.uk for information on the Education Act 1976, Chapter 81.
3. www.london.ac.uk/history.html. 1960s and 1970s history of education, including information on student numbers in UK universities.
4. Merton, R.K. (1949) *Social Theory and Social Structure*. New York: Free Press. A sociologist, Merton developed such notable concepts as 'self-fulfilling prophecy'.
5. Rosenthal, R. and Jacobson, L. ([1968, 1992] 2003) *Pygmalion in the Classroom: Teacher Expectation and Pupils' Intellectual Development*. Carmarthen: Crown House Publishing.
6. Richard Bandler and John Grinder are the co-inventors of neuro-linguistic programming (NLP). See www.richardbandler. com/Neuro-linguisticprogramming and wwwjohngrinder.com.

7. O'Connor, J. and McDermott, I. (2007) *An Introduction to NLP: Psychological Skills for Understanding and Influencing People.* London: Thorsons [audio CD].
8. Linley, P.A. and Joseph, S. (2004) *Positive Psychology in Practice.* New York: Wiley.
9. *European Year for Active Ageing and Solidarity between Generations: Report for the European Commission 2012.* Available at: www.dwp.gov.uk/policy/ageing%2Dsociety/european%2Dyear%2Dfor%2Dactive%2Dageing/. With the aim of promoting active ageing and doing more to mobilize the potential of the rapidly growing population in their late 50s and over, across Europe.

Chapter 5

1. Kline, N. (2009) *More Time to Think: A Way of Being in the World.* Pool-in-Wharfedale: Fisher King Publishing.

Chapter 6

1. Hamilton, J.-A. (2010) *Starting a Business Later on in Life.* Available at: www.businesswings.co.uk/articles/Starting-a-business-later-on-in-life. Businesswings provides news, articles, business ideas, information on starting a business, and administrative advice. Figures quoted are from research by PRIME – Prince's Initiative for Mature Enterprise – information on setting up a business. See www.prime.org.uk.
2. Information from a series of reports by Future Foundation for the press and consumers on behalf of Friends Life. Pension reform, ageing and retirement, health and wellbeing, employment. Available at: www.visionsofbritain2020.co.uk/.
3. Statistical information provided by Age UK. Information and advice for the elderly. Default retirement age, redundancy, and business success. Available at: www.ageuk.org.uk.
4. Martin Zwilling (www.startupprofessionals.com/), nurturing the development of entrepreneurs. Providing first-hand mentoring, funding assistance, and business plan development.

Chapter 7

1. See www.legislation.gov.uk for information on the Pensions Act 2011.

Chapter 8

1. ICM poll for Age UK, 13–15 January 2012. See www. icmresearch.com.
2. For information on the Gary Craig Emotional Freedom Technique, see www.emofree.com.
3. Diagram from Smedley, K. (2008) *Who's That Woman in the Mirror? The Art of Ageing Gracefully*. London: Headline Springboard.

Chapter 10

1. See the government website www.statistics.gov.uk for information on age composition, marriage, births, divorce, etc.
2. Saga (2010) *Sex and Money to Blame for Rising Tide of Over 50s Divorce*. Available at: http://www.saga.co.uk/money/news/sex-and-money-to-blame-for-rising-tide-of-over-50s-divorce.aspx.
3. Office for National Statistics (2011) *Civil Partnerships in the UK, 2010*. London: ONS. Available at: www.ons.gov.uk/ons/rel/vsob2/civil-partnership-statistics--united-kingdom/2010/index.html. Provides data on partnerships formed and dissolved in the UK, information, legislation and procedures relating to civil partnership statistics. The Act in full can be found at: www.legislation.gov.uk/ukpga/1967/60/pdfs/ukpga_19670060_en.pdf.
4. Office for National Statistics (2010) *Marriages in England and Wales, 2010*. Available at: http://www.ons.gov.uk/ons/rel/vsob1/marriages-in-england-and-wales--provisional-/2010/marriages-in-england-and-wales--2010.html. See also Beaujouan, E. and Bhrolcháin, M. (2011) Cohabitation and marriage in Britain since the 1970s, *Population Trends*, 145: 35–59.

Chapter 11

1. Alzheimer's Society (2012) *Statistics*. Available at: www. alzheimers.org.uk/site/scripts/documents_info.php? documentID=341. Includes infographic showing the key dementia statistics.
2. Report by the AA (2000) *Helping the Older Driver*. Available at: www.theaa.com/public_affairs/reports/heling_the_older_driver.pdf.
3. See www.warwick.ac.uk/newsandevents/pressreleases/aging_ overweight_people. Study, published in March 2002, led by Warwick Medical School at the University of Warwick. The study examined lifestyle and health patterns in more than 10,000 people in the USA and UK and their links to participants' mental and physical quality of life and health status.
4. A topical application of plant extracts containing xanthine derivatives that can prevent UV-induced wrinkle formation. R&D Division, Kose Co. Ltd., Tokyo, Japan. See www.ncbi. nim.nih.gov/pubmed/17523930.
5. Global Insight, Inc. (2007) *A Study of the European Cosmetics Industry: Executive Summary*. Report prepared for the European Commission, Directorate General for Enterprise and Industry. http://ec.europa.eu/enterprise/newsroom/cf/_getdocument. cfm?doc_id=4561.
6. ResPublica (2011) *Age of Opportunity: Older People, Volunteering and the Big Society*. Report written by ResPublica Associate Antonia Cox, in conjunction with Independent Age. Available at: www.respublica.org.uk/documents/how_ResPublica%20 Age%20of%20Opportunity%20Executive%20Summary.pdf.
7. World Health Organization (2012) *10 Facts on Ageing and the Life Course*. Geneva: WHO. Available at: www.who.int/ features/factfiles/ageing/en/index.html.

Chapter 12

1. Quote taken from Trotsky's *Diary in Exile*, written in 1935 and published in 1958.

2. See de Castella, T. and Brown, V. (2011) Why can't we imagine ourselves getting old?, *BBC News Magazine*, 5 August. Available at: www.bbc.co.uk/news/magazine-14412025. Christensen, K., Doblhammer, G., Rau, R. and Vaupel, J.W. (2009) Ageing populations: the challenges ahead, *The Lancet*, 374(9696): 1196–1208.

3. Rock, D. (2009) Managing with the brain in mind, *Strategy + Business*, Autumn, Issue 56. Available at: http://www.strategy-business.com/article/09306?gko=5df7f.

4. Isaacowitz, D.M. and Blanchard-Fields, F. (2012) Linking process and outcome in the study of emotion and aging, *Perspectives on Psychological Science*, 7(1): 3–17.

5. Information on loneliness taken from Weiss, R. (1975) *Loneliness: The Experience of Emotional and Social Isolation*. Cambridge, MA: The MIT Press.

Chapter 13

1. Quote by Oscar Wilde, a nineteenth-century Irish writer, responding the word 'assumption'.

Bibliography

Aspey, L. (2011) Time for a rethink? New pathways for executive development, *Developing Leaders: Executive Education in Practice*, 5: 44–8.

Bandler, R. (2005) *The Secrets of Being Happy: The Technology of Hope, Health and Harmony*. Massachusetts: I.M. Press, Inc.

Bandler, R. (2008) *Get the Life You Want: The Secrets to Quick & Lasting Life Change*. London: Harper Element.

Benson, H. (2003) *UK Marriage Statistics*. Available at: http://www.2-in-2-1.co.uk/ukstats.html.

Beaujouan, E. and Bhrolcháin, M. (2011) Cohabitation and marriage in Britain since the 1970s, *Population Trends*, 145: 35–59.

Bevan, R. and Wright, T. (2005) *52 Brilliant Ideas – Unleash Your Creativity*. Oxford: The Infinite Ideas Co., Ltd.

Brown, P. and Hales, B. (2011) Neuroscience: new science for new leadership, *Developing Leaders: Executive Education in Practice*, 5: 36–43.

Christensen, K., Doblhammer, G., Rau, R. and Vaupel, J.W. (2009) Ageing populations: the challenges ahead, *The Lancet*, 374(9696): 1196–1208.

Craig, G. (2011) *The EFT Manual (Everyday EFT: Emotional Freedom Techniques)*, 2nd edn. Fulton, CA: Energy Psychology Press.

De Bono, E. (1995) *Serious Creativity: Using the Power of Lateral Thinking to Create New Ideas*. London: Harper Collins.

Dilits, R. (1990) *Changing Belief Systems with NLP*. Capitola, CA: Meta Publications.

Doran, G.T. (1981) There's a S.M.A.R.T. way to write management's goals and objectives, *Management Review*, 70(11): 35–6.

Dyhouse, C. (1995) *No Distinction of Sex? Women in British Universities, 1870–1939*. London: Routledge.

Eales-White, R. (1994) *Creating Growth from Change: How You React, Develop and Grow*. Maidenhead: McGraw-Hill.

Feinstein, D., Eden, D. and Craig, G. (2006) *The Healing Power of EFT and Energy Psychology*. London: Piatkus.

Gillard, D. (2011) *Education in England: A Brief History*. Available at: www.educationengland.org.uk/history.

Goleman, D. (1996) *Emotional Intelligence: Why It Can Matter More than IQ*. London: Bloomsbury.

Gottman, J.M. (1994) *Why Marriages Succeed or Fail and How to Make Yours Last*. New York: Simon & Schuster.

Groves, D. (2004) *Stress Reduction for Busy People: Finding Peace in an Anxious World*. Novato, CA: New World Library.

Hamilton, J.-A. (2010) *Starting a Business Later on in Life*. Available at: www.businesswings.co.uk/articles/Starting-a-business-later-on-in-life.

Hayman, S. (2005) *Stepfamilies: Surviving and Thriving in a New Family*. London: Simon & Schuster.

Holden, R. (1999) *Happiness Now! Timeless Wisdom for Feeling Good Fast*. London: Hodder Mobius.

Hunt, S. (2009) *Family Trends*. London: Family & Parenting Institute.

Isaacowitz, D.M. and Blanchard-Fields, F. (2012) Linking process and outcome in the study of emotion and aging, *Perspectives on Psychological Science*, 7(1): 3–17.

Klett-Davies, M. and Skaliotis, E. (2009) Mothers, childcare and the work–life balance, in S.A. Hunt (ed.) *Family Trends: British Families since the 1950s*. London: Family and Planning Institute.

Kline, N. (1999) *Time to Think: Listening to Ignite the Human Mind*. London: Cassel Illustrated.

Kline, N. (2009) *More Time to Think: A Way of Being in the World*. Pool-in-Wharfedale: Fisher King Publishing.

Larcom, M.J. and Isaacowitz, D.M. (2009) Rapid emotion regulation after mood induction: age and individual differences, *Psychological Sciences and Social Sciences*, 64B(6): 733–41.

Lewis, T., Amini, F. and Lannon, R. (2001) *A General Theory of Love*. New York: Vintage Books.

Lingren, H.G. (1991) *Myths and Facts about Aging*, Children and Family Report. Honolulu, HI: University of Hawaii at Manoa, Institute of Tropical Agriculture and Human Resources (CTAHR), Brief 099, CF-14. Reissued November 2006 at: http://www.ctahr.hawaii.edu/freepubs.

Linley, P.A. and Joseph, S. (2004) *Positive Psychology in Practice*. New York: Wiley.

Locke, A. and Latham, G. (1989) *A Theory of Goal Setting and Task Performance*. London: Prentice-Hall.

Luengo-Fernandez, R., Leal, J. and Gray, A. (2010) *Dementia 2010: The Prevalence, Economic Cost and Research Funding Compared with Other Major Diseases*. Report produced by the Health Economics Research Centre, Department of Public Health, University of Oxford for the Alzheimer's Research Trust. Available at: http://www.dementia2010.org/reports/Dementia2010Exec Summary.pdf.

MacLean, P.D. (1990) *The Triune Brain in Evolution: Role in Paleocerebral Functions*. New York: Springer.

McKenna, P. (2012) *I Can Make You Smarter*. London: Bantam Press.

Merton, R.K. (1949) *Social Theory and Social Structure*. New York: Free Press.

Milne, C., Milner, J. and Van Norman, K. (2001) *Global Population Ageing: Peril or Promise?* World Economic Forum. Vancouver: ICAA Services, Inc.

O'Connor, J. and McDermott, I. (2007) *An Introduction to NLP: Psychological Skills for Understanding and Influencing People*. London: Thorsons [audio CD].

O'Connor, J. and Seymour, J. (1990) *Introducing Neuro-Linguistic Programming: The New Psychology of Personal Excellence*. Detroit, MI: Aquarian Press.

Rock, D. (2009) Managing with the brain in mind, *Strategy + Business*, Autumn, Issue 56. Available at: http://www.strategy-business.com/article/09306?gko=5df7f.

Rosenthal, R. and Jacobson, L. ([1968, 1992] 2003) *Pygmalion in the Classroom: Teacher Expectation and Pupils' Intellectual Development.* Carmarthen: Crown House Publishing.

Simring, S., Simring, S.K. and Busnar, G. (1999) *Making Marriage Work for Dummies.* New York: Wiley.

Smedley, K. (2008) *Who's That Woman in the Mirror? The Art of Ageing Gracefully.* London: Headline Springboard.

Smedley, K. (2009) *Who's That Sleeping in My Bed? The Art of Relationships for Grown-ups.* London: Headline Springboard.

Smedley, K. and Whitten, H. (2006) *Age Matters – Employing, Motivating and Managing Older Employees.* London: Gower.

Smith, T. and Harper, J.P. (2007) *When Your Parent Remarries Late in Life: Making Peace with Your Adult Stepfamily.* Cincinnati, OH: Adams Media Corporation.

Spencer, S. (2005) *Gender, Work and Education in Britain in the 1950s.* Basingstoke: Palgrave Macmillan.

Street, C. (2010) Application of neuroscience in executive team coaching: the WSR case, *NeuroLeadership Journal,* 3: 64–77.

Walmsley, B. (2006) *Teach Yourself Life at 50 – For Women.* London: Hodder Headline.

Ware, B. (2011) *The Top Five Regrets of the Dying: A Life Transformed by the Dearly Departing.* London: Hay House.

Weiss, R. (1975) *Loneliness: The Experience of Emotional and Social Isolation.* Cambridge, MA: The MIT Press.

Whitman, P. (1953) *Speaking as a Woman.* London: Chapman & Hall.

Index